Woman's Legacy

BETTINA APTHEKER

Woman's Legacy

Essays on Race, Sex, and Class

in American History

The University of Massachusetts Press

Amherst 1982

Acknowledgment is made to the following publishers for permission to
reprint from material under copyright.
Freedomways, 799 Broadway, New York, N.Y., for J. H. O'Dell, "Charleston's Legacy to the Poor People's Campaign" (reprinted from *Freedomways* 9, no. 3 [1969]); The Johns Hopkins University Press for Martin Kaufman, "The Admission of Women to 19th Century American Medical
Societies," *Bulletin of the History of Medicine* 50 (1976); The University of
Chicago Press for Ida B. Wells, *Crusade for Justice*, ed. Alfreda M. Duster,
© 1976.

For Jennifer, Joshua, & Lisa
who shall inherit

Contents

Acknowledgments

The idea for this book grew out of the research for my master's thesis. My work was a comparative study of the labors of Ida B. Wells and Mary Church Terrell, two women who helped shape the main contours of the civil-rights movement in the United States in the twentieth century.

Without the support of the faculty, staff, and students at San Jose State where my thesis was done, these essays could not have been successfully written. Phillip Wander, Marie Carr, and Herbert Craig, from the Department of Speech-Communication, served on my thesis committee and provided me with their collective historical and critical wisdom.

Billie Jensen, one of the first on our campus to develop the field of women's history, also served on my committee. Beyond this formal role, Billie has been a personal and intellectual inspiration. Her criticisms of this manuscript in various stages of its completion and her cheerful, almost daily counsel for three years have been indispensable. In short, she was my mentor.

Carlene Young, the chair of the Afro-American Studies Department at San Jose State, provided me with a steady source of material, enlightenment, and encouragement as this work progressed. She secured permanent status for a course on Afro-American women in history and arranged for me to teach this class under the auspices of the Afro-American Studies Department.

With their love, confidence, and support my colleagues in the Women's Studies Program at San Jose State University made this work possible. I am particularly indebted to Sybil Weir, Ellen Boneparth, and Selma Burkom who, as the respective coordinators of the program during my years at San Jose State, encouraged me to teach new courses, the research for which produced much of the material included in the last two chapters of this book.

I have also received additional and significant validation of my work. Another abridged version of my essay on W. E. B. Du Bois was published in San Jose Studies in May 1975, and it was also presented to a forum on the life of

Dr. Du Bois held at the University of San Francisco in the spring of 1979 under the auspices of the American Institute for Marxist Studies. My work on Du Bois was greatly helped by my participation in a graduate seminar at San Jose State on modern Afro-American history taught by Gloria Alibaruho.

My essay on Black women in the professions was originally prepared for the Fourth Berkshire Conference on the History of Women and presented at Mount Holyoke College, South Hadley, Massachusetts, in August 1978. My essay on lynching and woman suffrage was presented at the First National Scholarly Research Conference on the History of Black Women, sponsored by the National Council of Negro Women in November 1979. Finally, I am indebted to the faculty in the History of Consciousness Program at the University of California, Santa Cruz, where I am a doctoral student, for providing me with the time and support to complete the introductory essay and the final revisions in the manuscript. I especially thank Barbara Epstein, Donna Haraway, and Diane Lewis for their supportive readings.

For the location of otherwise unobtainable materials I am indebted to the staffs of the interlibrary loan services at both San Jose State and the University of California, Santa Cruz; Shirley Soldin of the documents division in the library at the University of California, Santa Cruz; Joan Densmore, director of the Seneca Falls Historical Society, in Seneca Falls, New York; Robert H. Land, Juanita D. Fletcher, and John C. Broderick of the manuscript division of the Library of Congress in Washington, D.C.; and Jacqueline Goggin of the National Archives of Black Women's History headquartered at the National Council of Negro Women in Washington, D.C.

I also wish to express my appreciation to Alfreda M. Duster for her assistance in my research on Ida B. Wells. Mrs. Duster, the youngest daughter of Ida B. Wells, and her sister, Miss Ida Barnett, welcomed me into their Chicago home and allowed me access to their mother's papers both at home and at the Regenstein Library at the University of Chicago. Mrs. Duster took me on a tour of Chicago in which her own vivid recollections of the Black community provided many missing links of people and places in my research. She also gave me a deep sense of history and community. My friendship with Mrs. Duster and Miss Barnett has been one of the enduring pleasures of this and related projects.

Various people have read all or parts of this manuscript and have provided me with detailed critiques. I am particularly grateful to Fanieul Rinn for her appraisal of the battle over the Fifteenth Amendment and her knowledge of constitutional law; to Renate Bridenthal, for her careful reading of the entire manuscript and her excellent suggestions transmitted from New York City in long letters with page-by-page notations; and to my mother, Fay P. Aptheker, who has read everything I have ever written with scrupulous and enthusiastic attention, and whose revolutionary partisanship makes such readings a political necessity and a personal delight.

The work of my father, Herbert Aptheker, in Afro-American and Civil War history provided the major theoretical grounding for the first two essays. His reading of the manuscript produced many helpful criticisms. I am most grateful, however, for his patient discussions with me while I was attempting to clarify my thinking around the issues of the nuclear family, reproduction, and domestic labor.

Ellen Timothy read every essay in this collection from the earliest moments of each conception. Her attention to historical detail, interpretive nuance, feminist process—in short, to the physical creation of the intellectual enterprise —made this work an increasingly instructive and joyful project.

Without the friendship of Leone Stein of the University of Massachusetts Press, who encouraged me to submit the manuscript to the Press, it is likely that publication of this book would have been greatly delayed. She has remained actively engaged with the project ever since, and her recommendations have been invaluable. I am also indebted to John Brigham of the Political Science Department of the University of Massachusetts, Amherst, for his helpful reading, and to Kathleen Barry who served as our consulting editor. From her initial reading of the manuscript as a referee for the Press, to her work with me in the editorial realm, Kathy has been as steadfastly supportive of the project as she has been rigorous and demanding in her interpretation of women's history. Her work on the life of Susan B. Anthony provided me with original and valuable insights.

Finally, I express my gratitude to Kate Miller for her excellent reading of the manuscript in the last stages of its evolution and for her patient attention and daily counsel during the process of revision and completion. Her confidence in me and in this work made its publication possible.

Bettina Aptheker
Pacific Grove, California
September 1981

Woman's Legacy: A Beginning

"ELECTRA Speaks," subtitled "a work in progress," was performed in an old warehouse converted into a theater on West 52nd Street, a few blocks from the Hudson River, New York City. The play was written by Clare Coss, Sondra Segal, and Roberta Sklar, and performed by the Women's Experimental Theatre, "committed to the creation and performance of theatre that reflects the experience of women. . . ." It was an extraordinary evening. The Greek tragedy hitherto portrayed in a patriarchal rendition of war, vengeance, and incest (or variations on one or more of these themes à la Ibsen and Sartre) was transformed into a forum for woman's mutilated voice, rising with cautious wisdom above the din.

The play began with a scene called "Matrilineage." Each performer introduced herself to the audience: "I am Sondra, daughter of Lille, daughter of Sarah Rebecca, daughter of Tzvia, daughter of a woman from Austria." No woman could go back more than two or three generations, and last names were frequently unknown. Along the wall in the corridor of the theater was hung a huge piece of butcher paper. Pens were provided and women were encouraged to write their matrilineage on the paper. Many had already done so. I wrote: "Bettina, daughter of Fay, daughter of Sara, daughter of Bella, daughter of a woman from the Ukraine."

The First National Scholarly Conference on the History of Black Women was held in Washington, D.C., in November 1979, under the auspices of the National Council of Negro Women. In existence for forty years, with a membership of 800,000, the Council is one of the oldest and largest women's organizations in the United States. Fifteen hundred people attended the conference, ninety percent of whom were Black women.

It was, I calculated to myself, the 106th year of emancipation. I could assume, therefore, that the woman Frances seated next to me at the banquet table, with whom I chatted through dinner, who was the mother of two small children, was the daughter of a woman whose mother had been a slave. I saw then, confirmed in the arrangement of matriliny, that for the women around me, and for millions around all of us, slavery is neither remote nor obscure. It is, in a profoundly intimate sense, a family affair. I recalled Sheila Rowbotham's thought that "the intimate oppression of women forces a redefinition of what is political and what is personal."[1]

The overriding theme of the conference, presented in clear and unmistakable detail, was that for Black women racism and male supremacy have been and remain inseparable realities. Liberation from one is not possible without confronting and overcoming the other. By focusing attention on the female experience we begin to understand the way in which racial oppression and the national oppression of a people intersect the patriarchal and capitalist structure in a definitive way. The Black female experience, by the very nature of its extremity, illuminates the subjugation of all women. In the United States, at least, we may project the conclusion that the emancipation of woman is inseparable from the liberation of Afro-American people in general, and the Afro-American woman in particular.

Slowly too, there was the dawning of a new consciousness in the work of the conference, a tentative and compelling conclusion. This was that the liberation of Afro-American people cannot proceed without the simultaneous dismantling of the male supremacist edifice. This idea will necessarily create a whole new way of thinking about class, race, and sex.

On the afternoon of the first day we heard presentations on Black women, racism, and the American legal process. Pauli Murray, one of the senior female attorneys in the country, told us a story which has stayed with me. Thirty years ago, Murray was just out of law school, the only woman in her graduating class at Howard. After great difficulty she secured a job with a New York law firm, and one of her first clients was a woman from Spanish Harlem, who was accused of prostitution. The case went to trial, and the chief witness for the prosecution was the "john." The prosecutor elicited every detail of the sexual transaction and in conclusion asked the witness to identify the woman with whom he had had this sexual association.

Without a moment's hesitation the witness identified Pauli Murray.

The Washington audience gasped, of course, as she told the story, and then we started to laugh. Pauli Murray laughed with us, saying she could laugh thirty years after the fact, but still, she wanted to be sure that we understood the complete humiliation to which she was subjected. When she rose to move dismissal of the case, the judge ordered her seated, denied the motion, found the woman from Spanish Harlem guilty, and sentenced her to a prison term.

It occurred to me later how hard it had been for Pauli Murray to tell us that story, even after thirty years.

Mary Berry, an assistant secretary in the Department of Health, Education and Welfare, delivered a detailed legal-historical analysis of the antimiscegenation laws. The kernel of her analysis lay in showing the connection between racism and male supremacy. The antimiscegenation laws were intended, of course, to proscribe the sexual turf of the Black male. At the same time, the Black woman in slavery remained beyond the pale of civil-rights or legal protection, and coexistent with the antimiscegenation laws in the Southern states was the legalization of her rape.

On the morning of the second day we came to the paper by Thavolia Johnson of Purdue University on Black females and the slave narratives. All attention was focused on the female experience under slavery, about which, we were informed, we knew virtually nothing. Nothing. In examining the narratives, almost all of which were written by men, in seeking clues to the female expression, we hear in a new way the words of the ancient survivor who in the thirties was interviewed by a researcher under the auspices of the WPA. The survivor said, "I'll give you somethin' for your book, but I ain't goin' to tell you everythin' I seen, or everythin' that happened, 'cause I don't want to think about it no more, and 'cause you won't believe me if I tell."

It is precisely here—at the juncture of the racist and male supremacist terror rooted in her class position—that the Black woman sustained the devastating blows of a double bondage as woman/slave and chattel/slave. She survived. But we do not yet have the record of woman's self-conscious articulation of her survival. "All silence has meaning," Adrienne Rich wrote.[2] The articulation is coming, and in the final instance it will determine the theoretical and practical limits of the female experience.

The women whose labor produced this conference are, above all else, lovers: of race, of children, of Black men, of each other. One was struck by the displays of affection incorporated into the everyday work of the conference, of woman's embrace of woman, of the sustained applause of collective solidarity transcending racial bounds so that I too was welcomed, my labor cherished, my personhood acknowledged.

The fruits of the civil-rights movement of the sixties were harvested at the Shoreham Hotel in Washington. These were women who had held onto the principle of affirmative action, fought for its implementation, learned in battle-scarred classrooms, and never left the communities of their birthing. They were about the business of determining self, scraping away the residue of centuries of racist/sexual encrustations, and naming their matrilineage in authentic and exquisite detail.

Out of the civil-rights/antiwar cataclysm of the sixties, a mass-based women's movement arose in the United States. It has been about the business of naming itself, of breaking silence, of creating a cultural matrix from which to articulate the meaning of woman's experience. It has challenged both the patriarchal and class relations of property which for so long have determined woman's destiny. Women of all races and national origins have inscribed its purposes. Its quintessential demand has been for equality.

In claiming equality with men, feminists in the last half of the twentieth century have begun to allow us to see women as a force coequal with men across the historical terrain. As feminists who have a commitment to Marxist theory and Socialist praxis, the assumption of equality between women and men in the historical process has demanded a re-examination of the parameters and structure of Marxist thought itself.

A feminist vision in modern times is one in which the concept of equality goes well beyond the notion of legal, political, and economic equality between women and men. In a modern sense, the concept of equality is a transformative one, a revolutionary idea. It means that women will have at least as much as men to say about everything in the arrangement of human affairs. In short, "feminist" in the modern sense means the empowerment of women.

For women of color, such an equality, such an empowerment cannot take place unless the communities in which they live can successfully establish their own racial and cultural integrity—unless racism can be overcome. The experiences of women of color must assume a cocentral focus in the shaping of feminist thought and action. Without this the liberation of women cannot be either envisioned or realized.

The use of materialist thought in feminist analysis has been essential because a materialist approach assigns woman's condition to history rather than to "nature." It insists that the source of woman's oppression must be rooted in the social conditions of each particular historical period. The tendency of men toward dominance, violence, and aggression is, likewise, historically rooted and not a "natural" or "essential" disposition. A materialist approach, therefore, also confirms that what was socially constructed in one way can be changed to another.[3] Adrienne Rich is correct when she reminds us that "the feminist politics of the past have been turned back over and over again because we had no overall understanding of the transitory nature of patriarchy, and no means of articulating and handing-on a collective female vision."[4]

It is difficult for both women and men to understand the transitory nature of male supremacy precisely because it does permeate all our institutions and all areas of life, and is especially pervasive within the family. It appears to be a natural ordering because it has existed for so long and in such varied forms. Indeed, it is believed to have its material origins in, and may have affected the assumption of, class rule itself. It is, therefore, not only an ideological question or cultural manifestation, but it is rooted in the social and economic fabric of civilization.[5]

This male supremacist structure predates recorded history. It is assumed in the societal imposition of the family under male hegemony and enforced in the social construction of sexuality and maternity. It is embedded in the archeological ruins of antiquity and in anthropological theory pronouncing the origin of "Man." It is transmitted in every currently institutionalized religion and philosophical system, and assumed in the structure of all known languages. For this reason, even the naming of woman's oppression is an exhausting enterprise.

The essays in this collection intend to interpret particular aspects of women's history in the United States. They focus on the history of Black women because the oppression of Afro-American people has been a central thread in the historical development of capitalism in the United States. The Black woman's experience, reflecting as it does a double proprietorship, clarifies the dialectical relationship between class exploitation and sexual oppression in a definitive way.

In writing this book I have also tried to show that the historical connection between Afro-American liberation and woman's emancipation does not depend upon the subjective consciousness of the participants in those movements. From a Marxist point of view, this relationship is an objective fact rooted in the historical development of capitalism in the United States, and in the idea that the struggle against racism is a central component of all revolutionary achievement. To the extent that participants in both movements have invoked a conscious collaboration, their mutual progress has been advanced. From this perspective too, we begin to see the extent to which ruling-class men have endeavored to divide these two movements from each other. Both racist ideology and patriarchal relations, which cross class and racial lines, have been used to break up this historic alliance.

I have been a political activist all my adult life. I was born into a Communist family and I have inhabited this world for as long as I can remember. My first demonstration was a picket line in front of a Woolworth's store in downtown Brooklyn in 1960 in support of the civil-rights sit-ins by Black students in the South. I was in Berkeley, California, through much of the sixties, and I began the seventies as a member of the national staff that conducted the legal and political defense of Angela Davis. It was my experience in the Angela Davis trial that propelled me into a study of Afro-American women's history and, ultimately, into women's studies.

Most of the essays in the present work were incited by

some aspect of my political activism—some strategic, tactical, moral, or personal issue which I attempted to clarify by working through what I thought might be an analogous historical process. This work then is not academic or scholarly in the sense of being remote from my life and my political and personal commitments. It is carefully researched and historically competent. But it is also partisan, activist, and inherently autobiographical. Indeed, I have ventured to make this intellectual process visible. Brief autobiographical comments appear at the outset of each essay. Finally, these essays were written for different occasions and purposes over a four-year period. Although they were not originally cast as chapters in a book, they do come together and are thematically and historically connected.

The present work engages a dialectical, historical-materialist mode of analysis. It also, however, tries to do something analytically new by placing women at the center of its attention. That is, I pose class questions from a woman's perspective, and I use woman's experience as the pivot from which to explore questions of class in a new way.

Having adopted an explicitly feminist perspective I have viewed women and men as equal forces in the making of history, and I have brought the social relations between the sexes into historical play.[6] That is, I have made apparently private affairs into a matter of political discourse. In these ways, I have attempted to contribute toward the arduous task of naming our oppression This is then an elaboration of our matrilineage, a chartering of woman's legacy.

2 Abolitionism, Woman's Rights and the Battle over the Fifteenth Amendment

Having been heavily involved in the student activism of the sixties I have an abiding interest in the texts that accumulated in its aftermath. As one of the leaders of the Berkeley Free Speech Movement at the University of California in 1964, I knew that I had forged at least a part of the history of those Berkeley days. Several other women also had been part of the recognized leadership of the FSM: Jacqueline Goldberg, Suzanne Savio, Beth Stapleton, Mona Hutchins. Hundreds of women had been active in the day-to-day life of the movement and arrested in the sit-in at Sproul Hall in December. Nevertheless, we found ourselves generally deleted from the histories of the movement.

As a partisan in the civil-rights and antiwar movements, moreover, I knew that hundreds, if not thousands of Black and white women had forged a significant part of the history of the sixties in general. The majority of published accounts—the anthologies, documentaries, essays and memoirs (including those of the Left)—were written by men, and these works placed men at the center of the politics and at the center of the experience. From this point of view, I knew that these works were only partial representations of a far more complex constellation of social and political experiences. There are exceptions to the male literary monopoly on the sixties, but a history of the period from woman's perspective remains to be written.

In reflecting upon this experience, I needed somehow to come to terms with our deletion as women. It seemed preposterous for me to write a history of the sixties in that sense, and I felt myself absurdly young to tackle a memoir. Still, I was trained as a historian. Surely there was a parallel movement, an analogous experience that would both clarify my own experience and bring a kind of personal satisfaction in claiming woman's historical record. Such was the immediate impetus for my connection to abolitionism.

I had a good background in abolitionist history, and I came to the material with a commitment to the centrality of the Afro-American freedom struggle to United States life and politics. As I resumed my connection with the standard and even revisionist historical literature, however, in search of a woman's perspective on the abolitionist experience, I was forcefully struck by two things: first, by the paternalism toward the women activists in the antislavery movement; and, second, by the implied and sometimes explicit criticism toward those apparently misguided or unduly excitable women who insisted on asserting the horror and degradation of woman's condition while slavery still prevailed.

Moreover, I was also struck by the omission of women's ideas and initiatives in the abolitionist movement, and by the almost total neglect of Afro-American women, with the exception of the ritual citations of Sojourner Truth and Harriet Tubman. The connection between abolitionism and the rise of a woman's rights movement was often confirmed but remained unexplored, as though it were peripheral to the main drama. There were and are exceptions to this general impression, and there is now a growing body of literature by women's historians. I consider and excerpt these in the essay that follows.

The point here is that the experience of researching another era, however perilous the historical analogy, confirmed my own lived experience in the sixties. It was important for me to have my perceptions of reality historically confirmed. As women we are so often accused of being self-centered, subjective, or trivial when we assert our significance however modest and tactful the assertion. When I turned to look at the experience of the abolitionist women a hundred years ago, I discovered more than a historical terrain. I learned also that criticisms of triviality and self-aggrandizement directed against us are often not personal counsels by "mature" historians, but political gestures that serve to conceal women's history and inhibit the process of reclamation.

RECOGNITION of the connection between abolitionists and the rise of a woman's rights movement in the United States forms a significant theme in feminist historiography. As Eleanor Flexner observed:

It was in the abolition movement that women first learned to organize, to hold public meetings, to conduct petition campaigns. As abolitionists they first won the right to speak in public and began to evolve a philosophy of their place in society and of their basic rights. For a quarter of a century, the two movements, to free the slave and liberate the woman, nourished and strengthened one another.[1]

Historians generally confine the relationship between the two movements to a twenty-five-year period, commencing in 1848 when the first woman's rights convention was organized at Seneca Falls, New York, and terminating with the split in the Equal Rights Association in 1869 over the proposed support for the Fifteenth Amendment to the United States Constitution, providing for Black male suffrage. The Equal Rights Association, organized by Susan B. Anthony and headed by Elizabeth Cady Stanton and Frederick Douglass, represented the organizational fusion of the abolitionist and woman's rights movements after the Civil War.

In granting the franchise to Black men alone, the Fifteenth Amendment necessarily implied a constitutional intent not to extend it to women. For this reason, members of the Equal Rights Association were divided over endorsement of the amendment, and some, led by Stanton and Anthony, actively opposed its passage. This split effectively ended the organizational viability of the Equal Rights Association, and the alliance between the two freedom movements.

There is considerable literature on this division in the Equal Rights Association, much of it sympathetic to the Stanton-Anthony position. A racist current is also often evident in this literature. Historian Alma Lutz, for example, in her biography of Cady Stanton, argues that the men who supported the Fifteenth Amendment did so because they "saw the rights of men as more important than the rights of women. And the rights of men in this instance meant the rights of male Negroes. The excuse given was political expediency. Little did it matter that Negroes were ignorant and utterly untrained in the principles of government. . . . The failure of the finest, most liberal men to understand women's position and humiliation taught Elizabeth and Susan a most valuable lesson—that women

*Abolitionism,
Woman's Rights,
the Fifteenth
Amendment*

could not depend on men for help in this matter—that they would have to fight their own battles."[2]

There has also been a more recent trend among feminist historians to conclude that abolitionism in general, and especially after the Civil War, had a primarily negative and regressive impact on feminism. Ellen DuBois, for example, in her study *Feminism and Suffrage*, takes the Lutz thesis a step further. Assuming that Stanton and Anthony advanced racist arguments in their opposition to the Fifteenth Amendment, DuBois maintains that "their break with abolitionists had freed them to investigate new aspects of the oppression and emancipation of women. As a result their feminism was becoming much more radical, especially with respect to sexual and economic issues."[3] Indeed, Ellen DuBois poses the break with abolitionism as the prerequisite for the emergence of an authentic, i.e., independent, women's movement in the United States.

Historian Aileen Kraditor, acknowledging the political expediency and acquiescence in racism by woman suffrage leaders after 1890, concludes that "if the suffragists of 1900 had defended the Southern Negro's right to vote ... they would have split the suffrage movement, destroyed its Southern wing, alienated many Northern supporters, and delayed passage of the Nineteenth Amendment [providing for woman suffrage]."[4]

Although Lutz, DuBois, and Kraditor have distinctive perspectives and purposes, they agree on two essential historical premises. First, they see abolitionism as a reformist rather than a revolutionary effort, and, second, they view the antislavery and suffrage organizations as essentially white. In this regard, it may be useful to separate the racist assumptions and conclusions of these writers from the actual historical record.

Cady Stanton and Susan B. Anthony especially had long and distinguished careers in the antislavery movement. Rather than assuming twentieth-century standards of racial etiquette and debate, it may be far more accurate to see Stanton and Anthony's anguish over the Fifteenth Amendment, and the anguish of their colleagues in the Equal Rights Association, which included Black women and men, in the light of that movement, and in the nineteenth-century context of racist and male supremacist ideology and practice.

In any event, the work of other historians, such as Eleanor Flexner, Gerda Lerner, Herbert Aptheker, Leon Litwack, and Rosalyn Terborg-Penn, and of scholars in other disciplines, such as Joyce Ladner, Dorothy Burnham, Angela Davis, and Johnnetta Cole, suggests the possibility of different conclusions.[5]

This paper begins an assessment of the abolitionist-woman's rights connection from a Marxist and a feminist point of view. In brief, it assumes that the issue of slavery and emancipation defined the contours of United States politics in the nineteenth century. It argues that abolitionism, by the very logic of its mission, became a revolutionary movement, unlike its reformist predecessors of the eighteenth century. Likewise, it suggests that emancipation was to have a profoundly progressive impact on the position of women in the United States.

The intersection of abolitionism and woman's rights in organization and personnel confirmed the revolutionary impulse of the antislavery cause. A mutually compelling dialectical arrangement sustained the two movements, so that each reinforced the radicalism of the other. The female presence helped to shape the revolutionary character of abolitionism and practical engagement in the struggle against slavery impelled a consciousness of a distinctly feminist vision.

This dialectical unity was effectively broken by the combined impact of racism in the women's movement, racist and male supremacist practices in the abolitionist ranks, and the machinations of Republican politicians, including abolitionist men, unwilling to support woman suffrage. Without such unity between the two freedom movements, woman suffrage was nearly lost on the altar of both white and male supremacy, feminist principles were badly damaged, and the civil-rights movement was severely weakened at a critical moment in its history.

The American and Female Anti-Slavery societies had three interrelated purposes: (1) the immediate abolition of slavery, without compensation to slave owners; (2) support for the civil rights of free Negroes, which included opposition to segregation and other racist practices and laws; and (3) assistance to fugitive slaves, which included provisions for the necessities of life, employment, and education, as well as aid in resisting slave hunters (includ-

Abolitionism,
Woman's Rights,
the Fifteenth
Amendment

ing United States marshalls in Northern states acting under authority of the 1850 Fugitive Slave Law).

The abolition of slavery as proposed by the antislavery organizations required the overthrow of the then-dominant section of the United States ruling class, the slaveholders. Although they were only a tiny proportion of even the Southern white population (in 1860 there were 175,000 slave owners in a Southern white population of 8 million), slaveholders represented the single greatest economic interest in the nation prior to the Civil War. From the founding of the Republic to the presidential elections of 1859, slaveholders were the controlling force in both major political parties, in all three branches of government, and in the armed forces. Further, abolition conjured the specter of Federal confiscation of nearly $4 billion in constitutionally protected, privately owned property. From a Marxist point of view, these facts augured the revolutionary implications of emancipation, which was the overthrow of the then-dominant section of the United States ruling class, the slave owners.[6]

To achieve such a revolutionary goal, a revolutionary movement was required, with a mass membership, an independent political base, a free press, a full-time cadre, and, ultimately, in the context of nineteenth-century realities, an armed force. Such was the character of the antislavery movement in the United States.

As it turned out, the course of emancipation was forced upon a section of the United States ruling class by military necessity; that is, a rising class of industrial capitalists, exhausted after two and a half years of civil war, had to undermine the political and economic foundation of its slaveholding adversary. But without the guiding vision, massive pressure, and armed assistance of the antislavery partisans, which included a quarter million Black men and women who fought in, serviced, and led guerilla actions for the Union army and navy, that ruling class would surely have staged a pathetic and partial rendition of emancipation.

The fact that this capitalist class later intervened in the Reconstruction of the former slaveholding states to abort the revolutionary process begun by emancipation explains the defeat of radical Reconstruction and the institution of the post-Reconstruction terror, but it in no way

diminishes the revolutionary quality of emancipation itself.[7] On the contrary, these facts illuminate the contours
of post-Civil War history, and the political forces arrayed
against the Fifteenth Amendment. It is precisely in apprehending the revolutionary quality of emancipation that
the battle over the Fifteenth Amendment may be finally
understood, and woman's legacy successfully charted.

From the beginning, women were part of the antislavery movement. They were present at the founding convention of the American Anti-Slavery Society (AASS) in
Philadelphia in 1833, and were among the most effective
organizers and orators on the abolitionist circuit. In his
autobiography, the Black abolitionist Frederick Douglass
assessed the role of woman's labor:

> When the true history of the antislavery cause shall be written,
> women will occupy a large space in its pages, for the cause of the
> slave has been peculiarly woman's cause. Her heart and her con-
> science have supplied in large measure its motive and main-
> spring. Her skill, industry, patience and perseverance have been
> wonderfully manifest in every trial hour. Not only did her feet run
> on "willing errands," and her fingers do the work which in large
> degree supplied the sinews of war, but her deep moral convic-
> tions, and her tender human sensibilities found convincing and
> persuasive expression in her pen and her voice.[8]

Woman's pen and voice, however, were not always welcomed into the abolitionist ranks. It violated all manner of
Victorian procedure for women to assume a public stance
on any issue, much less speak, petition, or organize in defense of it. More to the point, their activities undermined
the patriarchal structure of a society in which women had
been rendered the property of men. Unmarried women
and widows were the only members of the female sex
with a modicum of independent legal recognition.
Daughters and married women did not even receive their
own wages; if they were employed, their earnings went to
their fathers or husbands. Divorce could only be initiated
by the husband, who retained all the family's property
and custody of the children. Wife battery was legal, abor-
tion and even the advocacy of contraception, illegal. Rape
laws protected the rights of the male proprietor in his wife
or daughter, infanticide among working-class women
and the organized murder of the illegitimate babies of
middle-class women in orphanages through malnutri-

tion and infection were common practices. As a group, women were civilly dead and without political rights.

Although women were present at the founding meetings of the American Anti-Slavery Society and a few of them received permission to speak, they did not vote or otherwise partake in the decision-making apparatus of the convention. The AASS constitution provided that all persons except slaveholders, who subscribed to the organization's principles and supported it financially were eligible for membership. "For the first few years," one historian reported, "no one thought of defining 'persons,' and custom determined the respective roles of men and women members."[9] In time, however, woman's prominence in the antislavery work became evident. Lydia Maria Child, for example, was probably as important as William Lloyd Garrison in the formative years of the AASS; and by 1837 Angelina and Sarah Grimké were among the best known public figures identified with the abolitionist cause.

The notoriety given women by a generally hostile press provided proslavery forces with an added excuse to attack the AASS as a dangerous and subversive agency. Much opposition came from the churches. In 1837, a Pastoral Letter from the Council of Congregationalist Ministers of Massachusetts, then the largest denomination of the state, was widely circulated. The Pastoral Letter intoned against the unwomanly and unchristian behavior of the antislavery women.

The public controversy affected the internal life of the antislavery societies. What had begun as a relatively minor question of constitutional form and personal custom now loomed as a major political contest, in which several other issues would be simultaneously resolved.

In the spring of 1838, women were given permission to participate equally with men in the proceedings of the New England Anti-Slavery Convention. Several men objected, and some withdrew their membership. The following spring, under the leadership of the Reverend Amos A. Phelps, a rival, the Massachusetts Abolition Society, was created, the specific purpose of which was to exclude women from its proceedings. The main core of the New England society, however, remained intact. Other splits occurred in various localities, with similar results.

Forced by public denunciation and private criticism to defend themselves, abolitionist women asserted their equality with men, and proclaimed their right to organize, petition, and speak in behalf of a just cause. Angelina Grimké wrote:

> We cannot push Abolitionism forward with all our might *until* we take the stumbling block out of the road. . . . You may depend upon it, tho' to meet *this question may appear* to be turning out of our road, that *it is not.* IT IS NOT: we must meet it and meet it now. . . . Why, my dear brothers can you not see the deep laid scheme of the clergy against us as lecturers? . . . If we surrender the right to *speak* in public this year, we must surrender the right to petition next year, and then the right to *write* the year after, and so on. What *then* can woman do for the slave, when she herself is under the feet of man and shamed into *silence?*[10]

While the struggle had taken its toll on the women involved, it had also served a vital political function. Those in the AASS who had opposed woman's equality were equally conservative on the issue of slavery. Some approved of gradual rather than immediate emancipation and others were attracted to a variety of colonization schemes which sought to remove the Negro from the United States. Their defeat on the woman question helped to weaken the imposition of their political views on the whole work of the society. .

Furthermore, abolitionists had learned that they would have to do constant battle for their right to speak and publish their views in a country where pulpit, press, and ruling class were of or sympathetic to the slaveholders. William Lloyd Garrison was almost lynched in Boston in 1834, others were regularly mobbed, whipped, and otherwise abused. Elijah P. Lovejoy was murdered in Alton, Illinois, in the winter of 1837 for publishing his antislavery *Observer.* To restrict the activities of a portion of their own membership was simply to undercut the essential democratic premise of the abolitionist commitment. Indeed, as one scholar concluded:

> The natural and inevitable result of the argument between abolitionists and their opponents was to make rights, not only ideas, the point of conflict. The insistence upon the moral and legal rights of a minority to speak and be heard, with full protection from suppression or interference, became in time nearly as important as the abolition of the slave system. . . . The abolitionists

and those in the North whose sympathies led them to see slavery as a threat to freedom, eventually united to protect those elementary rights, basic to a democracy, by abolishing slavery.[11]

Women were at the cutting edge of the battle for civil liberties from the beginning.

Finally, the assertion of woman's equality was an essential step in making the AASS a truly mass organization. A theory of organization was implemented that tolerated the most diverse views and opinions within the abolitionist movement. Members had only to subscribe to the society's views on the question of slavery to be welcomed. This unity and mass base were achieved in spite of the fact that there were many splits and factions which plagued the antislavery movement over the years. This included the jockeying of male leaders, especially for positions of power and political favor in the Republican Party, and a sectarianism that sometimes isolated the AASS from potential support. Sectarianism was especially a problem with someone like William Lloyd Garrison who was opposed to the United States Constitution because he believed it to be *essentially* a proslavery document. Garrison argued that by establishing the slave as three-fifths of a man for purposes of congressional representation, and in other ways protecting property relations, the Constitution sanctioned and enforced slavery. Garrison was countered in these views by many, including Frederick Douglass, who believed that while Garrison's points were well taken, the Constitution implied a revolutionary ethos which made slavery an anathema to it.

The struggle for woman's equality within the abolitionist ranks marked a historic turning point in the growth of a self-conscious movement for woman's emancipation in the United States. The experiences within the AASS had convinced many women that the launching of a specifically Female Anti-Slavery Society would have a singularly beneficial effect on the whole movement, and would increase the capacity of the women to fully engage their energies.

The first such effort resulted in the organization of the Philadelphia Female Anti-Slavery Society, founded only a few months after the AASS. One of its main organizers was Lucretia Mott, who recalled later that, at the time of the founding, she had no idea of how to conduct a meeting. She said she had "no idea of the meaning of preambles and resolutions and votings." Women were seldom in assemblies of any kind and she had attended only one other convention before, "of colored people in this State." She reported that at the founding meeting of the Philadelphia group there "was not a woman capable of taking the chair, [and] organizing that meeting in due order, and we had to call on James McCrummell, a colored man, to give us aid in the work."[12]

The founding Convention of the national Female Anti-Slavery Society was held in New York City in May 1837. Committed to both the abolition of slavery and the equality of women, the delegates embraced Black women as equal members, concluding that "those societies that reject colored members, or seek to avoid them, have never been active or efficient. . . ." The women denounced race prejudice and called for racial integration of churches and schools. They further attacked the complicity of Northerners in the return of fugitive slaves and called for jury trials for alleged fugitives.[13]

The Female Anti-Slavery Society was the first national woman's rights organization in the United States. It was composed of Black and white women, and Black women made up a significant part of its leadership, notably in Boston and Philadelphia. Sara Parker Remond, Charlotte Forten, Sarah Mapps Douglass, Letetia Still, the Forten sisters (Margaretta, Harriet, and Sarah), among others, joined forces with white women such as Lucretia Mott, Abby Kelley Foster, and Maria Weston Chapman to organize the collective labors of the antislavery movement.

With the organization of the Female Anti-Slavery Society, the questions of woman's equality was no longer posed in moral terms of abstract justice. Equality had been elevated to the realm of practice. It had been a requisite objective enabling women to join in the urgent and all-consuming tasks of abolition. But the practical experience would in its time lay the foundation for a theoretical leap into feminist consciousness.

Indeed, the essay by the Southern-born abolitionist, Sarah Grimké, *The Equality of the Sexes and the Condition of Women* (Boston, 1838), represented, in the opinion of historian Eleanor Flexner, the first serious discussion of woman's rights by an American woman. Sarah Grimké argued for social, political, economic, and legal equality between the sexes. She condemned the rape of Black women under slavery and observed the injurious effects of that system upon the white women of the South. Likewise, she pointed to the effects of inequality upon marital relations, portending the future content of the feminist claim:

That there is a root of bitterness continually springing up in families and troubling the repose of both men and women, must be manifest to even a superficial observer; and I believe it is the mistaken notion of the inequality of the sexes. As there is an assumption of superiority on the one part, which is not sanctioned by Jehovah, there is an incessant struggle on the other to rise to that degree of dignity, which God designed women to possess in common with men, and to maintain those rights and exercise those privileges which every woman's common sense, apart from prejudices of education, tells her are inalienable; they are a part of her moral nature, and can only cease when her immortal mind is extinguished.[14]

By 1840, the American antislavery movement was committed to women's equality, at least in organizational principle. There were now 1,350 local societies, with a combined membership of a quarter million. In that year a World Anti-Slavery Convention was organized in London, England. That convention was to advance the cause of the slave and, unintentionally, advance the cause of woman as well.

The world meeting focused attention on the need to end the slave trade. Although declared illegal by both the American and British governments early in the century, the trade had continued illegally, profitably, and under the most barbarous conditions. The delegates concluded that unless slavery itself were successfully attacked on a world scale—and they had in mind the American South in particular—the slave trade could not be ended. This represented an important advance in a world movement that had previously shunned interference in the internal affairs of another country by isolating the issue of trade from the institution of slavery itself. Furthermore, "the convention represented an attempt to strengthen and enlarge the crusade against slavery by drawing together into one combined effort the abolitionist forces of the mid-nineteenth century. . . . The meeting marked the beginning of the sustained movement toward international organization. . . ."[15]

There were 520 delegates and "admitted visitors" including fifty-three Americans. Women were a significant part of the United States delegation. Among them were Lucretia Mott, Sara Pugh, Abby Kimber, Emily Winslow, Ann Green Phillips, and Cady Stanton. The convention opened on June 12, 1840, in the Freemason's Hall, Great Queen Street, London. Almost immediately the issue of women's participation arose. It preempted all questions on the opening day and threatened to end the convention. The British hosts demanded that the American women be seated in the gallery and denied the right to speak or vote.

The American men rose in unison to defend their delegation. The British claimed that by excluding women they were sticking to the single issue of antislavery. Garrison's reply was that by excluding women "they did undertake to settle another great question." Another American pointed to the inconsistency of calling a world convention to abolish slavery, "and at its threshold depriving half the world their liberty." Wendell Phillips, whose wife was part of the American delegation, introduced a counter-motion that the women be seated as full delegates. He spoke:

It is the custom there in America not to admit colored men into respectable society; and we have been told again and again that we are outraging the decencies of humanity when we permit colored men to sit by our side. When we have submitted to brick-bats and the tar-tub and feathers in New England rather than yield to the custom prevalent there to not admitting colored brethren into our friendship, shall we yield to parallel custom or prejudice against women in Old England?

We cannot yield this question . . . for it is a matter of conscience. . . . We have argued it over and over again, and decided it time after time, in every society in the land, in favor of the women. . . . It is a matter of conscience, and British virtue ought not to ask us to yield.[16]

Despite the eloquent appeals, British delegates overwhelmed the American contingent, and the women were banished to the balcony. Phillips and Garrison joined them, in protest. Lucretia Mott attempted to organize a separate women's meeting, but was unsuccessful. And

Cady Stanton blazed: "[Abolitionists] would have been horrified at the idea of burning the flesh of the distinguished women present with red-hot irons, but the crucifixion of their pride and self-respect, the humiliation of the spirit seemed to them a most trifling matter."[17]

As a result of the London experience Stanton and Lucretia Mott resolved that, however long it might take, they would organize a woman's rights convention in the United States. Their resolve was realized eight years later, almost to the day, at a small Methodist Church in the town of Seneca Falls, in upstate New York. On that occasion 300 women, many of them veterans of the abolitionist war, adopted a Declaration of Sentiments for their own emancipation. Upon the second of the Black liberationist Frederick Douglass, they likewise endorsed Cady Stanton's motion that women seek the right to vote.

As circumstances forced the women to develop arguments in defense of their own rights, they evolved a core of radical ideas that penetrated deep into the abolitionist ranks. The heart of their analysis lay in extending the concept of equality to embrace all persons regardless of sex or race.

The two women most prominently associated with the abolitionist movement in its formative years were Angelina and Sarah Grimké. The sisters were from South Carolina, and reared in a well-to-do slaveholding family. Both abhorred slavery and had fled the South to avoid being witness to its cruelties. Compelled by conscience to publicly denounce the system they knew so well, the Grimkés became two of the most effective organizers in the service of the antislavery movement. As women they were a novelty in public appearances; as Southerners with a first-hand knowledge of slavery, they drew huge crowds. Of the two, Angelina was best known as a public speaker.

The Grimké sisters were officially engaged as agents of the American Anti-Slavery Society in New England in 1837. The following year, Angelina became the first woman ever to address a legislative body in Massachusetts. On February 21, 1838, at the Hall of Representatives in Boston, she presented members of the Legislative Committee with petitions bearing the signatures of 20,000 people urging the immediate abolition of slavery. The signatures had been secured by members of the Female Anti-Slavery Society in Boston.

During the same period, Angelina Grimké wrote the second antislavery tract to be published by a woman in the United States. *An Appeal to the Christian Women of the Southern States* was "a work unique in abolitionist literature because it is the only appeal by a Southern abolitionist woman to Southern women."[18] It presented a clear and reasoned argument extending the concept of equality to include Black people.

In redefining the bounds of egalitarian principle, Angelina was able to make the theoretical leap from the exclusively moral and religious invocations against slavery characteristic of eighteenth-century thought, to the revolutionary call for immediate abolition which animated the life of the nineteenth century. For in affirming the equality of Black people, Angelina insisted that they must, therefore, have a *natural* right to freedom. In this way, she evoked the doctrine that was a motive force of the American and French revolutions, as the philosophical raison d'être of emancipation:

It has been justly remarked that *"God never made a slave,"* he made man upright, his back was *not* made to carry burdens, nor his neck to wear a yoke, and the man must be crushed within him, before *his* back can be *fitted* to the burden of perpetual slavery; and that his back is *not* fitted to it, is manifest by the insurrections that so often disturb the peace and security of slaveholding countries. . . . Slavery always has, and always will produce insurrections wherever it exists, because it is a violation of the natural order of things, and no human power can much longer perpetuate it.[19]

In the *Appeal* Angelina further called upon Southern women to rise in opposition to slavery. She urged women to free any slaves they owned themselves and pay them wages; to petition their legislatures, even if they could only gather six signatures; to beseech their husbands, brothers, and sons to free their slaves; and to otherwise organize in public association with the antislavery cause. Angelina's *Appeal* was an anthem of Black emancipation. It was also an incitement to feminist revolt in that it urged Southern women to challenge the sanctity of male authority and property rights.

Attention to the egalitarian ethic made the women of the antislavery movement acutely conscious of racist practices in the Northern states. They frequently challenged these practices, most notably in the realm of public education. In this way too, they simultaneously advanced the rights of women to an equal education with men.

Prudence Crandall was a Quaker who ran a successful school for young girls in Canterbury, Connecticut, in the early 1830s. She employed a Negro servant, who encouraged her to accept a Negro girl, Sarah Harris, as a student. This child attended the Crandall school for only a short while, because an outraged citizenry forced the school's closing. But, in April 1833, the school reopened with the support of the abolitionist movement and the Black community in New England. Seventeen Negro children were recruited and enrolled as a representative group from several New England states.

Prudence Crandall was first threatened; then she was jailed for "harboring vagrants," i.e., her pupils. When these measures failed, the Connecticut legislature intervened. A special law was passed forbidding the harboring, boarding, or instruction in any manner or form whatsoever of any "person of color" not an inhabitant of the state "without the consent in writing, first obtained, by a majority of the Civil Authority, and also of Select Men of the town." Crandall was arrested, and tried three times before a conviction was finally secured against her. Her conviction in the third trial was a result of the judge's having held in his charge to the jury that Negroes were not citizens of the United States, even if they were free and lived in a free state. This charge presaged the notorious Dred Scott Decision by the United States Supreme Court twenty-four years later. Crandall's conviction was reversed in the Court of Errors, but on a technicality which did not challenge the judge's charge.

Throughout all this, Prudence Crandall kept her school open, but, finally, physical violence shut it down. The school windows were broken, manure dropped in the well contaminated the water supply, local storekeepers refused to sell food, and doctors denied their services. For eighteen months Crandall, her abolitionist supporters, and the Black parents held firm. But when the school was firebombed and the lives of the children endangered, they submitted to a bitter and agonizing defeat.

Prudence Crandall's trial was one of the most important cases in the history of the antislavery movement. In his outstanding account of this case, historian Dwight Dumond observes that "the Crandall case gave cohesion to anti-slavery principles" by forging a new consciousness of the issues of citizenship and civil rights for free Negroes in Northern states.[20] The struggle for education as evidenced in the Prudence Crandall case had engaged the energies of the Black community for many years.

Black parents had first petitioned for the desegregation of the Boston public schools in 1787. "We must fear for our rising offspring," the petition to the Massachusetts legislature read, "to see them in ignorance in a land of gospel light . . . and for no other reason [than that] they are black."[21] The petition failed, and the community established its own school in the basement of the African Meeting House.

Sixty years later in 1847 Benjamin F. Roberts filed suit in the Massachusetts courts in behalf of his daughter Sarah. He argued that she had to walk several miles to attend the "colored" school, each day passing the "white" school which was only a few blocks from her house. Accompanying the law suit was a public civil-rights campaign in which Black women were the driving force. William C. Nell, the recognized spokesman for the movement, reported: "In the dark hours of our struggle, when betrayed by traitors within and beset by foes without, while some men would become lukewarm and indifferent, despairing of victory; then, did the women keep the flame alive. . . . It was the *mothers* . . . who, through every step of our progress, were executive and vigilant. . . . It was these mothers who accompanied me to the various school-houses, to residences of teachers and committee-men, to see the laws of the Old Bay State applied in good faith."[22] The Massachusetts Supreme Court had finally ordered the desegregation of the Boston public schools, and, on September 3, 1855, "the colored children of Boston went up to occupy the long-promised land. . . ."[23] Between the defeat in Canterbury, Connecticut, in 1835 and the victory in Boston twenty years later, lay the back-breaking labors of the antislavery women and men. In those twenty years the balance of power had begun to shift in their favor.

Responding to the segregated facilities in most Northern cities, Black communities were forced to establish their own schools, libraries, and cultural centers. The 1,200 Black residents of Cincinnati, for example, opened a school for their children in March 1834. Within a year they had raised the funds to open three more schools, providing classes for both adults and children. Late in 1834 the youngsters at these schools were asked to write a brief essay on "What do you think most about?" Typical of the replies was this one, written by a twelve-year-old: "Dear school-master, I now inform you in these few lines, that what we are studying for is to get the yoke of slavery broke and the chains parted asunder and slaveholding cease forever. O that God would change the hearts of our fellow men."[24]

The child's vision poignantly illustrates that in the Black community the struggle for education was part of the struggle against slavery. A great many of the Black women who labored in the antislavery movement were also teachers.

One of the first women to speak publicly in the United States, Maria W. Stewart, was a Black schoolteacher. Addressing wide audiences at the African Masonic Hall in Boston, in four lectures between 1832 and 1833, she advocated both the abolition of slavery and equality for women. The poet, orator, and novelist Frances Ellen Watkins Harper, who wrote the first novel ever published by a Black woman in the United States, was a teacher. The militant journalist, Mary Ann Shadd, was also a teacher. She organized fugitive slaves in Canada, published her own newspaper, the *Provincial Freeman*, between 1851 and 1852, supported John Brown, raised the first colored regiment for the Union army in Indiana, and was the second woman of her race graduated from law school. The recording secretary for the Female Anti-Slavery Society in Philadelphia, Sarah Mapps Douglass, was the first Black woman awarded a medical degree, and was director of the Girl's Department at the famed Institute for Colored Youth in Philadelphia. She was responsible for introducing physiology into the girls' curriculum.

For these and hundreds of other Black women, the role of educator was more than respectable employment and a means toward an independent income, although, of course, these were important considerations in an era when few job categories were open to women. It was also an integral part of their commitment to liberation. They were working to guarantee that the future ranks of the antislavery movement would be endowed with an intelligent and commanding cadre.

Women first won the right to attend institutions of higher learning as a consequence of abolitionist agitation. A sit-in by students led by Theodore Weld in 1834 at Lane Seminary in Ohio resulted in the secession of the students from that institution, and the founding of Oberlin College. Oberlin admitted both Black people and women.

Racist laws and practices frequently intersected the patriarchal structure compelling the antislavery women to engage a simultaneous challenge. Such was the case in the effort to repeal the eighteenth-century Massachusetts statutes that prohibited "marriage and fornication between Negroes or Mulattoes and whites," and provided severe penalties for violators. The law was necessarily written as a general injunction, but it was primarily understood as a prohibition against relationships between Black men and white women, rather than as a protection for Black women against the violations of white men. The law was clearly intended to preserve the property rights of white men over their women. Women found these proprietary features of the marriage laws especially repugnant, and in the mid-thirties, Lydia Maria Child began the movement that was to culminate in their repeal almost a decade later.

Massachusetts women trudged through the streets of Boston, Lynn, Brookfield, Dorchester, Plymouth, and other towns, circulating a petition urging repeal of the laws. By 1840 they had succeeded in gathering over 9,000 signatures, two-thirds of them from women. Each year they presented their accumulated petitions to the Massachusetts legislature, and each year they were rejected in a hailstorm of vituperative comment. Accused of sexual indiscretion and promiscuity, the women persevered, and there were few defections from among the original signers. Persistent effort and growing public support forced

the repeal on March 10, 1843, of these eighteenth-century
statutes. Reporting the significance of this campaign, one
historian concluded: "The victory against the marriage
law had an important effect upon the anti-slavery movement and the history of Massachusetts. It gave the abolitionists a sense of their political power and capacity for
future success. It brought them new adherents in all sections of the population. It stimulated them to renewed effort against other forms of discrimination and segregation
—on the railroad, as well as in the churches, the schools
and the militia. . . ."[25] Moreover, this successful campaign
marked the first female challenge to the patriarchial
bounds of the marriage contract. In this regard too, the effort marked a historic turning point in the consciousness
of woman.

The campaign against the marriage laws was characteristic of women's participation in the antislavery movement. Perhaps in large measure because of their own
oppression and the limits it imposed on their personal
energies, women typically engaged in collective methods
of work, and endeavored always to marshall mass support. It was women who initiated a boycott of cotton and
other products made by slave labor. As the people responsible for the making of clothing, linens, sheets, and so
on, they were the main consumers of Southern-grown
products. The boycott was a logical, constructive, and direct action in which thousands could participate. The use
of petitions was a form of protest distinctly suited to the
kind of propriety demanded of even a rebel woman in the
Victorian era. It did not require an undue degree of personal exposure to circulate among friends, in private
homes, and at church gatherings. In this seemingly modest way, the antislavery women mustered tens of thousands of supporters. Commenting on her research experience, historian Eleanor Flexner reported that:

Today, countless file boxes in the National Archives in Washington bear witness to that anonymous and heart-breaking labor.
The petitions are yellowed and frail, glued together, page on
page, covered with ink blots, signed with scratchy pens, with an
occasional erasure by one who fearfully thought better of so bold
an act. Some are headed by printed texts, others are copied in
careful, stilted script, or in a hasty scrawl. They petition Congress
against the admission of more slave states into the Union—Flori-

da, Arkansas, Texas; against slavery in the District of Columbia; against the interstate slave trade; for the total abolition of slavery. They bear the names of women's anti-slavery societies from New England to Ohio.[26]

The petition campaigns placed women in an unexpected maelstrom of political controversy when in 1836 congressional authorities refused to accept them. The women then began an eight-year battle to establish the right of petition. South Carolina Senator John C. Calhoun led the movement to deny the right of petition to Congress on the matter of slavery. He argued that the petitions, in demanding the abolition of a form of property sanctioned by the United States Constitution, i.e., slaves, were unconstitutional on their face. Moreover, he said, slavery was a matter for state rather than federal jurisdiction, and, therefore, Congress had no authority to debate the issue.

Enforcing Calhoun's intentions, a South Carolina colleague, Senator Pickney, introduced a so-called gag-rule into the Senate. Imposed on May 26, 1836, it prohibited the submission of antislavery petitions to the Congress. Five successive congressional sessions endorsed similar restrictions.

Opposition to the slaveholding interests was led by the Massachusetts representative and former president of the United States, John Quincy Adams. He not only denounced slavery, but advanced progressive views on the right of women to engage in political activity.[27] Complementing the work of their congressional allies, the abolitionists launched a drive to garner national support for an unfettered right to petition. Women were again, in Douglass's words, "the sinews of war."

The battle was eventually won. The women's victory marked the moment when the American people established their absolute right to petition the government for a redress of grievances. It also marked the moment when the abolitionists won a critical claim of constitutional interpretation; namely, that slavery was a matter of national policy, under ultimate authority of the federal government. While Southern representatives adhered to "states' rights," and never acknowledged federal jurisdiction, decisive sections of the bourgeois government did. The acknowledgment advanced the struggle against slavery to a

Abolitionism,
Woman's Rights,
the Fifteenth
Amendment

broader and more intense level of political confrontation. Women had again been at the cutting edge.

In the process of attending to the needs inherent in appealing to public opinion for mass organization, women developed oratorical skills and literary eloquence previously untapped. The writings and speeches of Lydia Maria Child, Lucy Stone, Maria Weston Chapman, Mary Ann Shadd, Sara Parker Remond, Frances Harper, Anna Dickinson, Susan B. Anthony, Sojourner Truth, and Harriet Beecher Stowe reached tens of thousands and provided a strong counterforce to the prevailing proslavery winds. The militant underground activities of Harriet Tubman, Letetia Still, Laura Haviland, Susan Anthony, Ann Douglass, Catherine Delany, and Helen Garrison were yet another dimension of women's work, although their contributions were sometimes overshadowed because of their husbands' prominence in the movement. Looking at some of their lives and work is useful in appreciating women's compelling role in the antislavery cause.

The publication of Harriet Beecher Stowe's *Uncle Tom's Cabin* in 1851 was a crucial event in the history of antislavery. In a long essay on the life and work of Stowe, the Black civil-rights leader of post-Reconstruction times, Mary Church Terrell, wrote: "In estimating the value of *Uncle Tom's Cabin* it is not too much to say that the work of no writer of modern times has excited more general and more profound interest than did this masterpiece of Harriet Beecher Stowe. In recounting the incidents and in stating the reasons which led to the emancipation of the slave, it would be difficult to exaggerate the role played by this remarkable book."[28]

Uncle Tom's Cabin sold 300,000 copies in the United States alone in its first year of publication, and more than one and a half million in England. It was translated into more languages than any other book ever written, except the Bible and *Pilgrim's Progress*. Abolitionist writer Thomas Wentworth Higginson said of its author: "To have written at once the most powerful and contemporaneous fiction, and the most efficient antislavery tract is a double triumph in literature and philosophy to which this country has heretofore seen no parallel."[29]

Although Susan B. Anthony is most frequently identified with the woman's rights movement, her energies were devoted to both causes at the same time, and she was a spirited and dedicated activist in the antislavery movement for many years. Her father, Daniel, and her brothers, D. R. and Merritt, were also well-known antislavery partisans. The family home in Rochester, New York, was a frequent stop along the Underground Railroad, and was used especially after the Fugitive Slave Law was passed in 1850. Escaping slaves were secreted in the Anthony home and, with the guidance of Frederick Douglass and others, led on to Canada. Susan B. Anthony participated in all these activities, even as she was expected to perform the more traditional female roles of caretaker and cook for the Anthony household. Her brother Merritt fought with John Brown during the Kansas civil war in 1856, and her brother D. R. settled in Kansas with his family as part of the abolitionist move to make Kansas a free state, just before the outbreak of the United States Civil War.

Susan B. Anthony became the New York State organizer for the abolitionist movement, with the start of the 1860 presidential campaign. Under the Garrisonian standard of endorsing no candidate for the presidency because Lincoln's Republican Party platform promised only to prevent the expansion of slavery, while permitting it in the states where it existed, Anthony's slogan was: "No compromise with Slaveholders. Immediate and Unconditional Emancipation."

In her capacity as organizer, Susan Anthony toured New York State on the antislavery circuit. With the approaching turbulence of civil war, she confronted fierce violence from hostile mobs in every city where she appeared. In Buffalo, Rochester, Port Byron, Utica, Syracuse, and Rome it was impossible even to speak. In Syracuse, a mob dragged effigies of Anthony and local abolitionist Samuel J. May through the streets and then burned the mannequins. A public meeting was finally organized in Rochester at a Black church that opened its doors to Anthony in lieu of the regularly scheduled Sunday services. And in Albany a courageous mayor sat on the stage with a revolver laid across his lap all afternoon while Anthony successfully conducted two antislavery meetings.

Abolitionism, Woman's Rights, the Fifteenth Amendment

Anthony is primarily viewed as an immensely talented and effective organizer. She was. But her experience in the antislavery movement also established her as a first-rate orator with great personal courage and dignity. Further, as was true with many of the women in the movement, her antislavery views were well in advance of many of her white male colleagues, especially on the subject of Black civil rights and self-determination. Responding to critics of emancipation who questioned what would be done with the Negro, Anthony replied:

What will the black man do with himself, is the question for him to answer. I am yet to learn that the Saxon man is the great reservoir of human rights to be doled out at his discretion to the nations of the earth.

Do with the Negroes? What arrogance in us to put the question! What shall we do with a race of men and women who have fed, clothed, and supported both themselves and their oppressors for centuries. *Do* for the slaves? Why, allow them to do for us what they are now doing for Jeff Davis. . . .[30]

Along with her antislavery work and consistent with her views on self-determination, Anthony worked for legal reforms that would allow woman greater control over her own destiny. Early in 1860, Anthony and Cady Stanton assembled a woman's rights convention in Albany and successfully lobbied for passage of a property rights bill for women.

The law was in the form of an amendment to the New York State property law of 1848. Most of it was later repealed during the Civil War years when women's involvement in the war limited their continuing pressure on the legislature for these rights, but in its original form the 1860 law provided that women should control both inherited property and their own earnings. Further, married women could make contracts, sue or be sued, and establish their own businesses. Finally, the law held that "every married woman shall be joint guardian of her children with her husband, with equal powers regarding them." Recognition of Anthony's abolitionist heritage and attention to her contribution to abolitionist ideas and practice must be part of the context in which to view her post — Civil War actions in the Equal Rights Association and in the battle over the Fifteenth Amendment.

The former slave woman Isabella, who became the incomparable Sojourner Truth, was one of the oratorical geniuses of the abolitionist movement. Addressing frequently hostile audiences in states along the Southern frontier between 1843 and the Civil War, she won many a skeptic to the side of the slave and the woman. She was strikingly tall and handsome. Contemporary descriptions of her physical countenance, mental faculties, and personality coincide in all essential details. This tribute was written by a colleague a few months after her death:

She possessed a figure of remarkable muscular development, straight, gaunt, and nearly six feet in height. In color she was a full-blooded African; her eyes were large, brilliant and expressive; her voice strong, deep and masculine. Strikingly distinctive as was her personal appearance, it was excelled by the individuality of her character. She was endowed with a strongly imaginative nature which she ever held in proper check by shrewd common sense. Her fearless, regal mind bade defiance to the tyranny of slavery to make it servile; and all the bitter wrongs which she endured, failed to dull her keen sense of humor. Surrounded by circumstances tending to keep her in dense ignorance, her singularly alert mind had ever reached out to grasp every shred of knowledge which accidentally came in her way, and her tenacious memory proved so good a custodian of these treasures that she had at her command a fund which was a constant surprise to all with whom she came in contact. Most explicitly she always obeyed the voice of her conscience. Once convinced of what was right regarding any matter, she could not be induced to swerve from that side.[31]

Sojourner Truth's appearance before the woman's rights convention in Akron, Ohio, in 1851, in which she repeated the refrain "And ain't I a woman?," has deservedly become a landmark in historical and feminist literature. Less well known but equally apropos of her rhetorical genius was a speech before an antislavery convention in Ashtabula County, Ohio, in 1855. The abolitionist leader Parker Pillsbury, who was present on the occasion, wrote an account of the meeting. According to Pillsbury, a large number of proslavery advocates attended the Ohio convention intent upon its disruption. They were permitted to speak, and one young lawyer "arose to defend the church and the clergy. He said that negroes were fit only to be slaves, and if any of them showed intelligence it was because they had some white blood, for as a race they were but the connecting link between man and animals."[32] The young lawyer spoke for almost an hour, and his abusive and angry words threatened to turn the convention into a shambles. It was Sojourner Truth who rose to answer him:

She seemed almost to come up out of the depth of darkness or out of the ground. There she stood before us as a vision. Her tall, erect form, dressed in dark green, a white handkerchief crossed over her breast, a white turban on her head, with white teeth and still whiter eyes, she stood, a spectacle, weird, fearful as an avenger. . . . She spoke but a few minutes. To report her words would have been impossible. As well attempt to report the seven apocalyptic thunders. I have heard many voices of men and women, in a vast variety of circumstances on land and sea, but never a voice like hers then and there. She spoke not loud, nor in rage. She was singularly calm, subdued and serene. In her peculiar dialect and tone she began:

"When I was a slave away down there in New York, and there was some particularly bad work to be done, some colored woman was sure to be called upon to do it. And when I heard that man talking away there as he did almost a whole hour, I said to myself, here's one spot of work sure that's just fit for colored folks to clean up after."[33]

"The convention was a success," concluded Parker Pillsbury, "from that hour—and would have been a success with that scene alone."

No one more fully epitomized the revolutionary content of abolitionism or personified the emancipation of woman than the partisan who was known among her own people as Moses. Harriet Tubman, born a slave on the east shore of Maryland in 1820, personally led more than 300 men, women, and children to freedom along the Underground Railroad. She made nineteen trips into and out of the South, traveling over 1,000 miles each time through the rough and treacherous terrain of the Appalachian Mountains. Slaveowners offered a $40,000 award for her capture, but she was never taken.

However legendary she was as the master guide "who never lost a passenger," Harriet Tubman was infinitely more than a good "conductor" on the Underground Railroad. She was, above all else, a militant strategist with a clear and well-defined vision of what it would take to secure the liberation of her people. Her experience as a slave woman initiated the events that would lead to her strategic conclusions.

In 1844, upon her marriage to a free Black man named John Tubman, Harriet undertook an investigation into the legality of her own status as a slave. The significance of her inquiry lay in the fact that the law required that the children born of a slave were to assume the status of their mother. In this way white masters were allowed a sexual prerogative with slave women, without having to assume paternity, and the rape of Black women was institutionalized.

Harriet paid a local attorney five dollars and requested an examination of the last wills and testament of her mother's previous owners. She learned that her mother had been willed to her present owner on condition that she be freed at the age of forty-five. This provision was unknown to the mother and had not been honored.

When the price of cotton plummeted during a depression in the late 1840s, Harriet had good reason to believe that she would be sold. Fearing this, and having resolved that once free herself she would return to honor the freedom of her mother and the other members of her family, she fled: "I had reasoned this out in my mind: there was one of two things I had a right to, liberty or death. If I could not have one, I would have the other; for no man should take me alive; I should fight for my freedom as long as my strength lasted, and when the time came for me to go, the Lord would take me."[34]

With the help of a Southern white woman who ran a station on the Underground Railroad in Bucktown, Maryland, Harriet crossed over into freedom sometime in 1849. She recalled the moment: "I looked at my hands to see if I was the same person now I was free. There was such a glory over everything, the sun came like gold through the trees, and over the fields, and I felt I was in heaven."[35]

Harriet lived for a time in Philadelphia, and got a job as a cook in a hotel. Sometime in 1850, after the passage of the Fugitive Slave Law, she made contact with Harriet and Robert Purvis, organizers of the Vigilance Committee in Philadelphia's Black community. The Vigilance Committee was intended to protect the community from raids conducted by United States marshalls and slave hunters to capture alleged fugitives and remand them to slavery.

Through the Purvises, Tubman learned the details of the Underground Railroad. She returned to her old plan-

Abolitionism,
Woman's Rights,
the Fifteenth
Amendment

tation in Dorchester County, Maryland, in order to bring
out her sister, her sister's husband, and their two children. In the spring of 1851 she made another trip into the
South, and brought out one of her brothers and two other
men unrelated to her. A few months later she returned
again, this time to persuade John Tubman to come North
with her. He declined. She returned to the North accompanied by another group of slaves, although none of her
own kin was among them. Years later, under the most
dangerous conditions, she managed to bring out her
mother and father. But in the intervening time a broader
goal of general emancipation had presented itself to Harriet Tubman, and the legend of Moses was born.

In brief, her scheme was mass flight. It was not in con-
tradistinction to other forms of struggle, but was rather a
complement to the intervention of world public opinion
sought by the antislavery movement. Tubman's design
was intended to erode the economic foundation of the
slave system. Once the Civil War had begun, her dream
was realized as the slaves themselves fled the plantations
in overwhelming numbers. It was a movement which
W. E. B. Du Bois once described as a "mobile general
strike."[36]

Harriet Tubman was not alone in her idea of mass flight.
This was precisely the strategy of John Brown, and Harriet
was at least as important as the "Old Man" in planning the
assault on Harper's Ferry in October 1859. Only the combination of illness and Brown's decision not to further delay the attack prevented Tubman from assuming a public
role as the coleader of the uprising.[37]

Truly mass flight required the organization of fortifica-
tions along the hazardous routes of escape because fugitives would need food, clothing, shelter, and medical attention, and armed assaults by pursuing hunters would
have to be repulsed. In short, the flight of thousands demanded a guerrilla force capable of sustaining the most
basic needs of a great flowing stream of humanity. The essence of the Brown-Tubman plan seems to have been to
secure a position in the Loudoun Heights above the town
of Harper's Ferry, Virginia, and presumably proceed south
from there in careful stages, setting up armed fortifica-
tions along the way.

The town of Harper's Ferry was a splendid initial point

of attack from both a military and political view. As a military site the town was ideal; it was situated at the point where the Potomac and Shenandoah rivers meet. Across the Potomac was Maryland, the Allegheny Mountains and points north to freedom. Across the Shenandoah rose the Loudoun Heights, 500 to 700 feet above the town. They were the entrance into the Appalachian Mountains and points south. As a political target Harper's Ferry was also appropriate in that capture of its federal arsenal would dramatize the complicity of the government in the perpetuation of slavery and signal the serious intentions of those who had laid the siege.[38]

No one knew the Appalachian and Allegheny ranges better than Harriet Tubman; no one knew the rigors and complications of flight more thoroughly than Harriet Tubman; no one had a better estimate of the political pulse of the slave community than Harriet Tubman. She worked with such security in the months preceding the raid that even today, it is impossible to account for all her days. Her actual complicity in the attack was not discovered until an investigation by the United States Senate was conducted nearly a year later. Time has now further revealed how fully she collaborated with John Brown:

She gave sanction and association to conspiracy and insurrection when she believed that these methods were necessary to the freedom of her people. Brown found a personal inspiration in Harriet Tubman which few other living persons aroused in him. The highest expressions of admiration from him for another human being were spent upon her. She was "the woman" in whom he placed an implicit trust, the one person he admired above all other Abolitionists—"The General."[39]

A combination of unexpected circumstances and delays and the ultimately superior strength of the United States Marines who were summoned to quell the uprising led to Brown's defeat in the battle at Harper's Ferry; but the raid inspired thousands with the knowledge that the day of freedom was not to be long in coming. Awaiting execution at Charleston, Virginia, late in November 1859, John Brown penned a passionate defense of their action. His statement ended this way: "You had better—all you people of the South—prepare yourselves for a settlement of this question. It must come up for settlement sooner than you are prepared for it; and the sooner you commence that preparation, the better for you. You may dispose of me very easily—I am very nearly disposed of now, but this question is still to be settled—this Negro question, I mean. The end of that is not yet."[40]

In his biography of John Brown, W. E. B. Du Bois declared this final message to be "the mightiest abolition document." He was, Du Bois said, "the man who of all Americans has perhaps come nearest to touching the real souls of black folk."[41]

Brown certainly touched the souls of Black women, and many white women as well. While Harriet Tubman was most intimately tied into the conspiracy, other women were part of the plot. Mary Ann Shadd was almost certainly present in Chatham, Canada, in the spring of 1858 when the plans of attack were first laid. She also helped to publish the book, *A Voice From Harper's Ferry*, written by Osborne Perry Anderson, a twenty-four-year-old survivor of the battle.

Frances Ellen Watkins Harper was a close personal friend of the Brown family. She spent the two weeks prior to Brown's execution with his wife, Mary. And the legendary Mammy Pleasants, a wealthy, free Black woman from San Francisco, California, almost certainly financed a goodly portion of Brown's conspiracy and was herself in the South, disguised as a jockey, at the time of the raid.

Susan B. Anthony organized a memorial meeting in honor of John Brown in Rochester, New York, on the day of his hanging. Parker Pillsbury, then editor of the *Liberator*, agreed to deliver the main address. Anthony herself presided over the service when other antislavery leaders in the Rochester area would not do so, fearing for their safety should they be charged as coconspirators with Brown. She engaged Corinthian Hall and 300 people came. Anthony collected an admission fee on the advice of a Quaker friend who suggested that this would help to keep out hostile persons. Anthony sent the proceeds to the Brown family.

After John Brown's raid, and with the outbreak of the Civil War, Harriet Tubman went on to lend her considerable military and organizational talents to the United States Army. She raised colored regiments from among the fleeing slaves, operated an extensive and invaluable intelligence network, led commando raids on Confederate lines, and generally waged the war she knew would end in freedom. No other woman has ever played so prominent a role in the conduct of an American war, although she has received little recognition for that aspect of her remarkable career. Thirty-seven years after her war service, and only after special efforts were undertaken in her behalf, she received a small army pension in her own name.

After the war, Harriet Tubman settled in Auburn, New York. Although she lived in poverty, she used her home as a kind of settlement house for indigent Black folk. She peddled fruit and in other ways raised enough money to establish a more permanent "John Brown Home." She died in Auburn on March 10, 1913, in the fiftieth year of emancipation.

Two years into the Civil War, Elizabeth Cady Stanton and Susan B. Anthony summoned the "Loyal Women of the Nation" to convention at the Church of the Puritans in New York City. They resolved to gather a million signatures in the Northern states on a petition demanding the immediate abolition of slavery, with no compensation to slaveowners.[42] In practical terms this meant it would be necessary to obtain a signature from one in every twenty persons.

This campaign was conducted while riots against the military draft engulfed the city of New York. The draft act had been passed by Congress on March 3, 1863, and the women's convention was held in May. On July 11 the drawings for the draft commenced and, that night, the riots also began. For days marauding bands of whites attacked and hanged hundreds of Negroes, burned and looted federal and other buildings, beat and killed draft officials and antislavery people everywhere. An estimated 1,200 people were killed. An orphanage for Black children, one block from Stanton's house, was burned to the ground.

As was true for all abolitionists in the city, Stanton feared for her own life and for those of her family. Her son Neil was seized by the mob in front of the family home and only his own presence of mind saved his life. It was in this atmosphere, and in the aftermath of this violence, that the

Abolitionism,
Woman's Rights,
the Fifteenth
Amendment

women conducted their signature campaign. It fell to
Susan B. Anthony to keep the women's offices open and
the petitions moving.

Two thousand women worked fifteen months and secured 400,000 signatures. The first 100,000 were presented
to the United States Senate on February 9, 1864. The campaign continued through August. It was one year after the
Presidential Emancipation, and eighteen months before
ratification of the Thirteenth Amendment to the United
States Constitution abolishing slavery. By their actions,
the abolitionist women displayed an acute sense of interracial solidarity and class consciousness.

The end of the war confirmed the military defeat of the
Confederacy and the former slaveholding class, but no
revolution is exclusively a military affair. It is, above all
else, a political struggle. The transcendent political issues
facing the nation at the war's end were: What will replace
the old slaveholding order in the South? Who will determine its political principles and shape its economic and
social character? On what basis will federal troops be
withdrawn from the South and the colored regiments dis-
armed? Under what conditions will the Southern states
be readmitted to the Union? What is the position of the
newly freed slaves? Are they "persons"? Are they "citizens"? Should they exercise all the rights and privileges of
citizenship? Should they vote?

Black people held the balance of electoral power in the
South; and by their labor they held the balance of economic power as well. In Mississippi, five months after the
war, fifty-three percent of the potential electorate was
Black. In sections of Alabama and South Carolina Black
folk were likewise an absolute majority. Everywhere they
were the deciding minority. These facts loomed as issues
that would decide the future course of the American nation. This is the practical meaning of a conceptual framework that sees emancipation as a revolutionary event.
From this point of view, all social progress in the country,
including the progress of organized labor, populist farmers, and women, was bound up with the outcome of Black
Reconstruction.

Emancipation was a momentous occasion in the history of the Afro-American people. It was also a significant

event in the history of women. Emancipation brought with it the legal recognition of marriage between Black men and women. It ended the legally sanctioned rape of Black women, and the sale of tens of thousands of children. Moreover, the Black Reconstruction governments in the South, battling against time and with limited resources, sought to break up the landed, aristocratic rule of the old order. These governments attempted sweeping revolutionary changes that held important implications for the progress of woman.

The proslavery, racist regimes of the former slaveholding class were extremely reactionary on all questions, including the status of women. The Reconstruction governments, in contrast, advanced the position of women, by implication and design. In Mississippi, for example, the Reconstruction government took the following revolutionary actions during its all-too-brief tenure:

Property rights of women were recognized; imprisonment for debt was forbidden; a non-segregating public school system was provided for; local governmental organs were democratized, the judiciary was overhauled; the vote was given to all men over 21 years of age; and any and all discrimination by governmental units or private corporations on the basis of religion, color or previous condition of servitude was illegalized. . . . tax rates on tools and implements of mechanics and artisans were lowered. . . . Married women who worked, were to be paid their own wages directly and a married man could not sell his homestead without the consent and signature of his wife. Industrialization was encouraged. Railroad, banking, public utility, mining and manufacturing concerns were established as the state officials consciously strove to break the stranglehold of an agrarian, one-crop semi-feudal economy.[43]

In the meantime, on the national level, three constitutional amendments were introduced to fix the legal and political status of the newly emancipated slaves. The Thirteenth Amendment, ratified on December 18, 1865, abolished slavery. The Fourteenth Amendment, ratified on July 21, 1868, conferred the rights of citizenship, equal protection of the laws, and due process of law on "all persons born or naturalized in the United States." The Fifteenth Amendment, ratified on March 30, 1870, provided for Black male suffrage. By custom which had the strength

Abolitionism,
Woman's Rights,
the Fifteenth
Amendment

of law women did not have the right to vote. And, in 1872, Susan B. Anthony was arrested, tried, and convicted in New York State when she attempted to vote.

With the end of the Civil War, most of the antislavery societies dissolved themselves. With limited understanding of the dynamic of racism, many veterans of the movement believed that the crusade had come to an end. Susan B. Anthony, Frederick Douglass, Wendell Phillips, Cady Stanton, and others believed that, on the contrary, new initiatives and campaigns would have to be undertaken to secure the civil rights of the newly freed slaves and of women. Through the organizing skill of Anthony, the Equal Rights Association was founded in 1866. It was committed to advancing the civil rights of Black people and women. Anthony was secretary of the new organization, Cady Stanton was president, and Frederick Douglass was vice-president. This was the logical culmination of common struggle, a fusion cemented in the trauma of a thirty-year war for emancipation. But it was an alliance unable to survive the post—Civil War crucible of racism, male supremacy, and class collaboration. The first division came over the wording of Section 2 of the Fourteenth Amendment.

The Fourteenth Amendment granted citizenship rights to "all persons born or naturalized in the United States." Section 2 of the amendment provided that if the right to vote was denied or abridged "to any of the male inhabitants" of a state, that state's representation in the Congress "shall be reduced in proportion which the number of male citizens shall bear to the whole number of male citizens twenty-one years of age in the State."

The wording of Section 2 affirmed by implication that women did not have a legal right to vote in any of the respective states, and by introducing the word "male" into the Constitution this amendment would presumably prevent woman suffrage. Before women could vote it would have to be overturned or superseded by another constitutional amendment specifically granting women the vote. It could be reasonably interpreted, also, that state laws granting woman suffrage could now be declared unconstitutional. For these reasons Susan B. Anthony, Cady Stanton, Robert Purvis, Parker Pillsbury, and others in the

Equal Rights Association expressed great reservation and concern over the wording of the amendment.

The reason for Section 2, however, had nothing to do with the issue of woman's enfranchisement. Indeed, it is ironic but nonetheless probably true that the Republican framers of the Fourteenth Amendment did not even think about woman suffrage or the implications of introducing the word "male" into the Constitution until it was brought to their attention by the Equal Rights Association. The purpose of Section 2 in the amendment was altogether different.

At the time that amendment was drafted, the question of who voted and under what circumstances was fixed by each state. It was not a matter of federal jurisdiction, and suffrage was not construed as a constitutional right. Indeed, the United States Constitution makes no mention of suffrage, nor does the Bill of Rights. However, the Constitution did provide that representation in the House would be apportioned among the several states on the basis of the population of each state. For purposes of this count, it was constitutionally affirmed that slaves would be counted as three-fifths of a person.

With the abolition of slavery and the assumption of Black citizenship, the representation of the Southern states would have been substantially increased, because each Black person then constituted a whole for purposes of determining the number of representatives for each state. Fearful of the potential for increased Southern representation (which would ironically come to a defeated South still under the control of the former slaveholding class), congressional supporters of Reconstruction wrote Section 2 into the Fourteenth Amendment. They hoped then to devise a means of containing Southern influence and voting power in the House.

In other words, the Republican framers of the Fourteenth Amendment, whatever their Reconstructionist views, were also interested in Republican votes and partisan politics. The Democratic Party at this time controlled the votes of the former slaveholding class and, therefore, a goodly portion of the white South. The Republicans were trying to minimize the Democratic vote. Some constitutional authorities have also suggested that military necessities of the Union forces who were still occupying the South and were still dependent on Black troops compelled Congress to act on the Thirteenth, Fourteenth, and Fifteenth amendments.[44] It is yet an added irony that Congress has never enforced Section 2 of the Fourteenth Amendment and has never cut the representation of the Southern states, even though Black men were systematically and legally disenfranchised in every Southern state by the turn of the twentieth century. Here a complex of class forces aligned Southern dixiecrats with Northern financiers and industrialists against the laboring class and its Black component—an alliance that has forged Republican and Democratic party politics to the present day.

In summary then, the Fourteenth Amendment did not extend suffrage to anyone. It was not addressing the *right* to vote. It merely affirmed that if the Southern states should choose to prohibit Black men from voting, then Black people could not be counted in the population for purposes of representation. Note, of course, that the patriarchal assumptions of the framers of the Fourteenth Amendment rendered the Black woman constitutionally invisible!

With its important concepts of due process and equal protection, the Fourteenth Amendment was to lay the foundation for all the Supreme Court decisions relating to civil rights and affirmative action in the twentieth century. Moreover, and regardless of the intentions of its male authors, the amendment significantly if inadvertently advanced the position of women in that it recognized as "citizens" all "persons" born or naturalized in the United States. This was to become the explicit constitutional confirmation of female citizenship. Until passage of the Fourteenth Amendment the citizenship rights of women had been legally ambiguous. Because the law recognized married women as the property of their husbands, they were, by legal definition, "nonpersons" and married women had no civil rights. But these were all matters of constitutional interpretation in Supreme Court cases of the next century. There was no way for anyone, including the women and men in the Equal Rights Association, to have sorted through this legal maze or guessed at the ultimate court interpretations brought about largely as a result of mass movement for civil rights and women's rights in the middle of the twentieth century.

The constitutional significance of the Fifteenth Amendment was its assumption of federal jurisdiction in the matter of suffrage. In removing the right to suffrage from the control of individual states, the Fifteenth Amendment laid the constitutional foundation for universal suffrage. With its passage, women would be able to lay claim for the first time to another constitutional amendment for the same right, without regard to sex. This point was not lost on Susan B. Anthony, Frederick Douglass, or others in the Equal Rights Association. Anthony promptly proposed the drafting and submission to Congress of a Sixteenth Amendment for woman suffrage.

As had been the case a decade before in the prelude to the Civil War, Kansas was once again a testing ground, this time for both Black emancipation and woman's rights. On the November 1867 ballot the Kansas voters had before them two separate measures. One endorsed ratification of the Fifteenth Amendment. The other provided for woman suffrage in state elections. Lucy Stone, Frederick Douglass, Henry Blackwell, Susan B. Anthony, and Cady Stanton were the members of the Equal Rights Association dispatched to meet the Kansas challenge.

The Republican Party hierarchy, increasingly under the domination of industrialists and financiers, and fearing the radical import of a double victory in Kansas, split its endorsement of the proposed measures by abandoning woman suffrage. Wendell Phillips and Frederick Douglass tried to salvage an endorsement but it came too late and was too ambiguous to affect the outcome of the campaign, and most of the abolitionist men, deeply embedded in Republican politics, remained silent.

In the face of this desertion and fearing defeat for woman suffrage, Anthony and Stanton solicited support from Democratic Party leaders, who were delighted to split their Republican foes, even if it meant a temporary alliance with women. It was a truly desperate action, for Stanton and Anthony now found themselves in a political alliance with the party of the former slaveholders. They toured Kansas in the company of George Francis Train, a wealthy Democratic leader who was eccentric and erratic in his views and allegiances.

Abolitionism, Woman's Rights, the Fifteenth Amendment

Train wedded his support of woman suffrage to a compendium of issues that formed a kind of early populism that was on the one hand antimonopolistic, laissez-faire, agrarian, and capitalistic, and on the other hand, anti-Negro and racist. In return for his support, Stanton and Anthony remained silent on the issue of Black suffrage.

Both measures were defeated by the Kansas electorate. Black suffrage won 10,000 votes, and woman suffrage, 9,000. This was not a bad showing in an electorate that was white, male, and propertied. Cady Stanton was probably right when she said in retrospect: "I believe both propositions would have carried, but with a narrow policy, playing off one against the other, both were defeated."[45] Unfortunately, the Kansas lesson was not learned in time to affect the outcome of Reconstruction.

Stanton and Anthony continued their relationship with Train after the Kansas campaign. When he offered them money to publish their own newspaper, they took it. With Cady Stanton and Parker Pillsbury as editors, and Susan B. Anthony as the business manager, the *Revolution* made its debut in January 1868. It advanced many new and significant ideas on the oppression of women. It brought out the pervasiveness of woman's subordination and the scope of her servitude.[46] Cady Stanton's able hand addressed issues of suffrage, education, divorce, infanticide, battery, reproductive rights, and trade-union organization. The divorce question was especially controversial in the nineteenth century because it attacked a man's property rights over his wife and children.

But the paper also opened its pages to Train, who wrote a weekly column under a pseudonym in which he espoused his economic and political views; and the main editorial thrust of the *Revolution* was its opposition to the Fifteenth Amendment. The condition of Afro-American women, the struggle for civil rights and against the raging terror in the South went unreported and apparently unnoticed. Train presently lost interest in the paper and ended his financial support. Plagued with debts, the *Revolution* ceased publication in 1870.

The final split in the Equal Rights Association occurred at its New York Convention in May 1869. The issue at hand was whether or not the association should endorse the Fifteenth Amendment. Two resolutions were before the delegates. The Stanton-Anthony Resolution maintained opposition to the amendment: "Until the Constitution shall know neither black nor white, neither male nor female, but only the equal rights of all classes, we renew our solemn indictment against that instrument as defective, unworthy, and an oppressive charter for the self-government of a free people."[47]

Frederick Douglass offered a contrary proposal. The association, he said, "hails the extension of suffrage to any class heretofore disfranchised as a cheering part of the triumph of our whole idea . . . and gratefully welcomes the pending fifteenth amendment, prohibiting disfranchisement on account of race, and earnestly solicits the State Legislatures to pass it without delay."[48] Douglass went on to say that the amendment represented the "culmination of one half of our demands," and he called for the redoubling "of our energy to secure the further amendment guaranteeing the same sacred rights without limitation to sex."

Argument waxed eloquent on the motions. Stanton was of the opinion that the Fifteenth Amendment would set back woman suffrage a full century. Anthony said: "I will cut off this right arm of mine before I will ever work for or demand the ballot for the Negro and not the woman." Her sentiments were echoed by the Black abolitionist Robert Purvis, who asked how he could fight for the rights of his son without equally defending those same rights for his daughter. Frances Harper suggested that white women would place sex before race, but that as a colored woman she would have to let the "lesser issue of sex go," to champion the Fifteenth Amendment. Another woman, Mary Livermore, although white, agreed with and endorsed the Douglass approach. Henry Blackwell offered several motions similar to Douglass's, and strongly criticized the role of the *Revolution* in opposing Black suffrage.

Stressing the urgency of the Fifteenth Amendment, Douglass presented the most cogent appeal for its priority: "When women because they are women, are dragged from their homes and hung upon lamp-posts; when their children are torn from their arms and their brains dashed out upon the pavement; when they are objects of insult and outrage at every turn; when they are in danger of having their homes burnt down over their heads; when their

children are not allowed to enter schools; then they will
have an urgency to obtain the ballot."[49]

A woman in the audience called to Douglass: "Is that not all true about Black women?" Douglass replied: "Yes, yes, yes, it is true of the black woman, but not because she is a woman but because she is black."[50]

From the point of view of urgency, of course, Douglass was right, but Black women, as women, were also subject to special forms of racial and sexual oppression at the same time—a point Douglass had made on numerous occasions. Moreover, Douglass himself did not endorse the restriction of suffrage to men. His argument was compelled by the terror against Black Reconstruction then raging in the South. Lucy Stone came closest to expressing the dilemma confronting the men and women who debated this issue, and a dilemma it was, for she could not resolve the question of priority either:

Mrs. Stanton will, of course, advocate the precedence of her sex, and Mr. Douglass will strive for the first position for his, and both are perhaps right. If it be true that the government derives its authority from the consent of the governed, we are safe in trusting that principle to the uttermost. If one has a right to say that you cannot read and therefore cannot vote, then it may be said that you are a woman and therefore can not vote. We are lost if we turn away from the middle principle and argue for one class. . . . There are two great oceans; in the one is the black man, and in the other is woman. But I thank God for the XV Amendment, and hope that it will be adopted in every State. I will be thankful in my soul if *any* body can get out of this terrible pit. But I believe that the safety of the government would be more promoted by the admission of woman as an element of restoration and harmony than the negro. I believe that the influence of woman will save the country before every other power.[51]

Posed in terms of the priority of rights the debate over the Fifteenth Amendment was indeed insoluble. The only way to resolve the issue was to see it in terms of the future direction of the country. That is, the issue had to be viewed in strategic and historical perspective, in class terms, understanding the dialectical relationship between the two great movements for freedom.

The issue of Black suffrage was not the "Negro's Hour" in some abstract sense of moral righteousness, as though one oppressed group had a greater claim to right than another. On the contrary, Black suffrage was a strategic question forced by the particularity of historical circumstances in the United States. A Southern-based alliance of Black voters, the nonslaveholding mass of poor whites, and the merchant-artisan class of whites—which represented the composition of the Reconstruction governments—would have been able to sustain a progressive block that might have prevented the resumption of Bourbon rule.

Precisely because passage of the Fifteenth Amendment was intended to advance the cause of Afro-American freedom, it inevitably would have rebounded to the benefit of woman, but only a class-conscious element could have seen that point in 1869. Douglass and Stone came closest to understanding it, but neither one could develop an analysis that did not rest upon making one oppression more important than the other. And when a second motion was made to endorse the proposal for a Sixteenth Amendment granting woman suffrage, the motion was tabled and effectively quashed. This was done because a majority of the men in the Equal Rights Association were committed first to the pragmatic priorities of the Republican Party, and most did not see the compelling urgency of woman suffrage, or take women's oppression seriously. Indeed, many of them would have been themselves personally compromised had they done so.[52]

A majority of the Equal Rights Association delegates voted to support the Fifteenth Amendment, and Stanton and Anthony resigned their membership. They continued to advocate defeat of the Fifteenth Amendment, and maintained the National Woman Suffrage Association as a separate entity with little or no further interest in the cause of Afro-American freedom.

Others in the now dismembered Equal Rights Association formed a Boston-based American Woman Suffrage Association under the leadership of Lucy Stone, Henry Blackwell, William Lloyd Garrison, and Julia Ward Howe. Many of the Black suffragists joined the Boston group, and Frederick Douglass maintained membership in both the American and National suffrage associations. The American endorsed the Fifteenth Amendment and the principle of woman suffrage as a needed but not immediate reform. It also supported woman's educational and trade-

Abolitionism, Woman's Rights, the Fifteenth Amendment

union rights, but it shied away from the issues of divorce or reproductive rights. After ratification of the Fifteenth Amendment, however, the Boston-based group also abandoned the issue of Afro-American freedom. Later it opposed a federal amendment for woman suffrage, endorsing instead state-by-state campaigns as the exclusive route for suffrage.

With the break up of the Equal Rights Association, the essential unity of the two movements for Black and female equality had been ended. Had this unity not been broken it is possible that the women and men of the association would have been able to mount a defense of civil rights and for woman's rights comparable to the struggle they had waged against slavery. Had this been done the betrayal of Reconstruction would have at least been tempered by an organized opposition. But three factors had combined to prevent this unity. First, the majority of abolitionist men failed to maintain a political independence from the Republican Party. Although many were associated with the Republicans in order to work on civil-rights legislation and elect supporters of Reconstruction, they became committed to it in a way that prevented them from exercising independent judgment and actions. Second, with the ideological supremacy of patriarchal practices and values, woman suffrage and woman's oppression were seen as secondary and/or superfluous issues by many in the association. Third, racist ideology and practice led many to abandon prematurely the struggle for Afro-American rights once the Civil War was over, and racist assumptions propelled many women into ignoring or subordinating Black oppression in the face of their own.

As the woman's movement severed its self-conscious alliance with Afro-American freedom, it found itself without a progressive mooring. It is indeed interesting to witness the ways in which both Anthony and Stanton searched for a progressive linkage, especially through the working-class and trade-union movements of the time. It apparently never occurred to either of them that in the context of American politics, the neglect of or acquiescence in racism would inevitably force the women into a more and more conservative and politically ineffectual mold.

The politics of expedience that so characterized the National American Woman Suffrage Association after its reunification in 1890 was a direct consequence of racist practices that rendered Afro-American women and the Afro-American community invisible. NAWSA eventually turned on even its own radical mentors. At its 1896 convention a resolution was adopted disassociating the organization from the publication of Cady Stanton's *The Woman's Bible*. Stanton's biblical rendition was a brilliant and unrelenting indictment of the role of religion in the oppression of women.

However much they erred in the battle over the Fifteenth Amendment, Cady Stanton and Susan B. Anthony were towering figures in a revolutionary age. Each separately and both together made vital contributions to the abolition of slavery and the emancipation of woman. Stanton had an unsurpassed intellectual brilliance. In her writings and speeches she stripped away centuries of male supremacist assumptions and theories on religion, the family, sexuality, and politics. "She seemed," as one contemporary described her, "to live in several centuries at the same time."[53] Anthony, probably more than Stanton, had a passionate commitment to the antislavery cause, and a capacity for organization and perseverance unmatched in her day. She also had a primary commitment to, and a great love for, women. Above all else, she took woman's oppression seriously.

The point is not to defend or excoriate Stanton or Anthony. They were no more, and probably less, racist than many of their contemporaries in the abolitionist movement, although they have been more prominently rebuked. The point is to learn what we can from their experience and process. Neither one ever really *felt* the urgency, the pain, the dailiness of Afro-American oppression and struggle. Neither one ever grasped the extent to which the liberation of woman was bound up with the emancipation of the Afro-American woman and her people.

Susan B. Anthony had several significant relationships with Afro-American women, including Sojourner Truth, Ida B. Wells, and Mary Church Terrell. Evidence suggests that Sojourner Truth especially influenced her ideas. Overall, however, Anthony's role was of one soliciting Black support for woman suffrage without granting a re-

ciprocal support for Afro-American rights. Her relationships with Black women appeared to have been mutually
respectful and personally cordial.

Cady Stanton was lifelong friends with Frederick Douglass, and their relationship continued long after the battle
over the Fifteenth Amendment. Douglass never wavered
in his commitment to woman suffrage and he attributed
this to Stanton's abiding influence.[54] Indeed, the last day
of Douglass's life was spent at a meeting of the National
Council of Women in Washington, D.C. There is no evidence, however, to suggest that Stanton was ever influenced in the same way by Douglass on issues of emancipation and civil rights.

The apparent lack of reciprocity and equality in the relations Stanton and Anthony had speaks to a deep form of
white chauvinism which requires attention. It is a form of
omission and invisibility in which the ideas and experiences of Afro-American people are not accorded attention
or merit, in which they are not engaged as a serious perspective from which to view the world or the place of
woman within it.

The abolitionist struggle inspired the dawn of feminist
organization in the United States and the feminist ethos
infused the radical core of abolitionist thought and praxis.
We have much to learn from the revolutionary warriors of
the last century. We may celebrate the enchanting and
powerful vision of the Black and white women who fought
together for their mutual emancipation. We need also to
absorb deeply the recognition that woman's emancipation and Afro-American liberation are intimately and inexorably connected and that neither can ever be envisioned or achieved without the other. Our unity, however,
will demand a different order of politics, and a different
kind of process, in which themes of hierarchy, power, and
dominance are no longer tolerated, either personally or
politically.

3

Woman Suffrage and the Crusade
against Lynching, 1890 — 1920

*After having read Susan Brownmiller's history of rape,
Against Our Will, one scene played itself out over and over
again in my mind. Brownmiller described her experience
in going to the Schomberg Center for Research in Black
Culture, part of the New York City Public Library and
housed at 135th Street in Harlem. The center contains the
largest collection of material on Afro-American history, literature, and art in the United States. She asked the librarian for any material there might be on rape. The man returned with several boxes and folders on lynching. No,
Brownmiller said, she wanted material on rape. Lynching,
the librarian said, contained the material she wanted. They
went round and round like that. She looked at the material
on lynching, but did not find information on the rape of
Black women, which was what she was looking for.*

*The scene stayed with me because it illuminated the
problems of category, experience, and perspective that I
had experienced in my own work. For the librarian at the
Schomberg, the word "rape" immediately and appropri-
ately conjured the specter of lynching. For the young woman who had been repeatedly propositioned and harassed in
the streets and offices of New York City the word conjured
centuries of violence against women. The librarian at the
Schomberg and Susan Brownmiller stood apart, separated
in the first place by the chasm of history.*

*These were the thoughts that initially propelled me into
a study of lynching and rape. I wanted to assume a point of
view that would resolve the apparent contradiction between being able to resist the racist use of the rape charge
against Black men, and at the same time counter the pervasive violence and rape that affects women of all races and
classes. I knew from my own difficult and painful experiences that rape was a politically motivated act of violence
against women. I wanted to assume a point of view, therefore, in which there was no hierarchy of oppressions where
the violence against Black men was "more important" than
the violence against women, or vice versa; that is, a point of*

view in which lynching and rape could be seen as equally atrocious and politically connected acts of terror. I also felt there was an urgency to this question, expressed in the day-to-day politics, choices, and strategies of the women's movement.

It seemed logical to begin my search with what I knew, and so I reviewed the material on the antilynching crusade organized by Black women under the leadership of Ida B. Wells. Then I went on to read accounts of lynchings and the texts of congressional hearings and state commissions in which Black women testified to their own repeated violations by white men. I read all of this in small doses and then walked the stacks in the library or went outside so that I wouldn't throw up.

I continued the research by deciding next to look at the popular and scholarly literature produced by the established writers and intellectuals between 1890 and 1920. I was appalled at the crudeness of the racial and sexual assumptions. I remember clearly the moment—I was in the library staring off into space—when I saw the connection between lynching, rape, and woman suffrage. It was a historical connection, an interpretive connection that did not depend upon the consciousness of the women and men who struggled for suffrage and against lunching, but upon the point of view one realized with the material at hand.

The connection was made first on a relatively straightforward level when I saw that the category "suffrage" meant both Black suffrage and woman suffrage at the same time. Later, the insight took on layers of meaning for me. When I let go of the conventional use of the categories "lynching" and "rape," for example, it seemed to me that the antilynching crusade of Black women was also a movement—a Black women's movement—against rape. It was forged with the materials, resources, consciousness, and forms of argument and support that Black women had available to them at the turn of the century.

Conventional history puts "white men" at the center of its categories—and they are usually of the upper classes. Insofar as women's history replicates this pattern racially, it is frequently absorbed into or limited by its categories of analysis. The process I experienced in writing this essay was as instructive to me as the content. I learned that categories carried with them points of view that reinforced

themselves in cyclical persuasion. It was only when I was
willing to let go of the safety of old structures that I moved
forward. A similar process, I think, applies to politics.

TWO methods for achieving complete suffrage for
women were initiated in the United States. The first
strategy sought to gain the franchise for women state by
state. Between 1867 and 1910 many such campaigns were
conducted but only four were successful; between 1896
and 1910 no state campaigns won the vote for women.
The second method sought an amendment to the federal
Constitution granting women the right to vote. This
amendment process in the matter of voting rights was
made possible after the passage of the Fifteenth Amendment which provided suffrage for Black men. It was the
Fifteenth Amendment that introduced the idea that suffrage was a federal rather than a state right, for the original
United States Constitution makes no mention of suffrage
at all.

The two methods for achieving woman suffrage coex-
isted in the National American Woman Suffrage Association (NAWSA). Several important state campaigns were
conducted in California, New York, and Pennsylvania
after 1910. However, the practicality of concentrating all
resources in the battle for one constitutional amendment
moved that second strategy to the fore. Passage of the Anthony Amendment, named in honor of its author, Susan
B. Anthony, and granting women the right to vote, became
the cutting edge of the woman's movement after 1890.

The Southern-based Woman Suffrage Conference
(WSC), organized in New Orleans in 1913 under the leadership of Kate Gordon, however, rejected federal enfranchisement as a matter of principle, in favor of state's
rights. The state's rights argument was based on a constitutional assertion that only the respective states could set
qualifications for voting. This issue of constitutional interpretation had its origins among slaveholders in the ante-
bellum South, when the greatest fear had been federal intervention in the matter of slavery, but it continued after
the Civil War, as the former slaveholding class sought to
consolidate its power over the state governments.

Suffrage
and
Lynching

In the context of WSC's racist priorities, it was believed that the Southern legislatures would enfranchise white women if they could insure the continued disfranchisement of Black men, and the exclusion of Black women. By this logic, WSC assumed an antifeminist position and actually campaigned against ratification of the Nineteenth Amendment providing for woman suffrage.[1] It was for this reason that WSC did not affiliate with NAWSA. Although NAWSA was itself frequently ambivalent on the race issue, it denied funds to WSC and conducted its own rigorous campaign in the South. On the other hand, some of the influential leaders in WSC rejected Gordon's stand on the race question and personally associated themselves with NAWSA.[2]

The extension of suffrage to women, then, was intimately bound up with the endorsement of federal authority in the matter of voting rights and, consequently, the preservation and implementation of the Fifteenth Amendment guaranteeing Black male suffrage. Had the Fifteenth Amendment been rendered a nullity, the assumption of federal authority would have been seriously compromised. In that case, it is unlikely that a federal amendment providing for woman suffrage could have been won. However much sections of the largely white, upper-class leadership of NAWSA remained confused and ambivalent on the so-called Negro Question, it was to haunt the movement down to the last moments of its final triumph. The Black presence, both in the suffrage association and in the struggle for civil rights, contributed mightily to the woman's cause.[3]

For Afro-American people, the forty years preceding the passage of woman suffrage represented, in Rayford W. Logan's words, "the nadir."[4] With the end of Reconstruction in 1876, and the solid refortification of white supremacist rule in the South, special state laws were passed to institutionalize segregation and to prevent Black men from voting. Historian August Meier described the situation in the South this way: "By 1895 disfranchisement had been pretty well accomplished by various devices—legal and extra-legal—in most of the South; by 1908 another half dozen states had imitated Mississippi and South Carolina in enacting Constitutional provisions; and by

1915 practically all of the Southern states provided for white primaries. . . ."[5]

By the turn of the century, the repeal of the Fifteenth Amendment was under serious consideration. The intelligentsia condoned, encouraged, and sanctioned the disfranchisement of Black men. Professor James E. Boyle of the University of Wisconsin, for example, published an article in May 1904 entitled, "Has the Fifteenth Amendment Been Justified?," in which he concluded it had not. Boyle contended that until the Negro people learned to "build better and cleaner lives," and got "clear conceptions of right and wrong" the political franchise should not be granted. "The question is now," he concluded, "what shall be done with that dead letter, the fifteenth amendment?"[6]

Boyle's essay typified the veritable barrage of literary eloquence on the subject of Black inferiority and nullification that filled the pages of American journals between 1890 and 1920—not Southern journals, but national periodicals with tens of thousands of readers. The titles tell the tale: "Negro Suffrage a Failure: Shall We Abolish It?"; "The Black Shadow in the South"; "Have American Negroes Too Much Freedom?"; "The Race Problem: Disfranchisement As A Remedy"; "Shall the Fourteenth Amendment Be Enforced?"; "Negro Suffrage in the South"; "Shall the Negro Be Educated?"; and so on.[7]

Arguments sanctioning the de facto if not de jure nullification of the Fifteenth Amendment appeared in the academic journals as well. It was argued that although the Fourteenth and Fifteenth amendments granted the Negro political *rights*, they did not grant him political *equality*. In other words, discrimination based exclusively on the basis of race was unconstitutional, but discrimination on the basis of literacy, ownership of property, and taxation was constitutionally sound and morally imperative. In the words of one proponent of this view, writing in the *Annals of the American Academy of Political and Social Science* in 1906:

The negro as a negro has no longer any barrier placed in his path. He stands on the same footing as his fellow-citizens. The "inalienable rights" of the Declaration of Independence are for the first time recognized. No position short of these three amendments [the 13th, 14th, and 15th] could be logically or safely taken. They do not establish universal suffrage, they simply involve the doctrine that its conditions, whatever they are, shall be the same for all. Men as men shall stand on a fair footing with each other.[8]

Another scholar of the same period, writing a long account of the "History of Negro Suffrage" in the *Political Science Quarterly*, concluded: "Nor did the fifteenth amendment give him [the Negro] the right to vote; it merely invested the citizen of the United States with the right to be exempt from discrimination in the exercise of the elective franchise on account of his race, color or previous condition of servitude."[9]

In 1898, the United States Supreme Court affirmed the constitutionality of these interpretations of the Fifteenth Amendment. Two years after recognizing the constitutionality of segregation in its well-known case of *Plessy* v. *Ferguson*, the Court held, in *Williams* v. *Mississippi* (170 U.S. 213) that restrictions on the franchise were legally permissible, even though they might be applied primarily or even exclusively to colored people, as long as the language of the state law excluded the race issue per se. In the words of the Court: "Restrained by the Federal Constitution from discriminating against the negro as a race, the Mississippi Constitutional Convention discriminated against its characteristics and the offenses to which its weaker members are prone."[10]

While the debate on the legal interpretations of the Fifteenth Amendment proceeded, another commenced on the enforcement of Section 2 of the Fourteenth Amendment, that section that provided that the number of representatives in the United States Congress should be in proportion to the number of male citizens exercising the franchise in the respective states. Should any section of the male citizenry not vote, the state's proportion of representatives in the House should likewise be cut.

Arguing against enforcement of the Fourteenth Amendment, one Southerner candidly admitted that thousands of poor whites had also been disfranchised. Although directed against Black men, poll taxes, literacy tests, property ownership, and the "grandfather clause" that required proof that a male relative had voted in the 1860 presidential election (!) effectively excluded vast numbers of white voters as well. Still, this writer contended, the *quality* of the Southern ballot had been greatly enhanced, and surely the South should not be penalized for this:

> Not that the South desires the disfranchisement of any white man. The ties of race attachment are supremely strong. But through her awakening interest in popular education, the South testifies to her desire to bestow the qualifications for the ballot as well as the ballot, and to give suffrage by first fitting for suffrage. Is this double movement of beneficence to be arrested? Is the increasing interest in the qualification of our electorate and in the freedom of its leadership to be brought to disaster?[11]

The fact that Section 2 of the Fourteenth Amendment was never enforced assured Southern dixiecrats a powerful congressional position, by disfranchising their Black and poor white opposition and subjecting them to no penalty for this action. This is still a significant factor in American politics. Indeed, it was precisely the Southern influence that stymied the Anthony Amendment for woman suffrage. A reading of the *Congressional Record* between 1890 and 1918 shows that Southerners controlled both the House Judiciary Committee and the Senate's Woman Suffrage Committee. These men held the Anthony amendment in committee and off the floor of Congress for nearly thirty years.

Racist tracts in the scholarly and legal journals were matched by books and films which also received wide circulation: *The Negro: The Southerners Problem* by a popular Virginia novelist, Thomas Nelson Page (New York: Charles Scribner's Sons, 1905); *The Color Line* by William Benjamin Smith (New York: McClure, Phillips and Co., 1905), which W. E. B. Du Bois described as "a naked unashamed shriek for the survival of the white race by means of the annihilation of all other races";[12] *The Clansman* by Thomas P. Dixon (New York: Doubleday and Page, 1905), which ten years later was used as the basis for D. W. Griffith's technically sensational film, "Birth of a Nation," glorifying the birth of the Ku Klux Klan; *The Negro A Beast or In the Image of God* by Charles Carroll (St. Louis: American Book and Bible House, 1900), which argued from the scriptures that Black people were barely a notch above the chimpanzee on the evolutionary spiral. One of the leaders of the Anti-Imperialist League in the United States suggested that Carroll's work was "the most sacrilegious book ever issued from the press in this country." He re-

Suffrage and Lynching

ported that it was receiving "wide circulation among poor whites in the Cotton States" and concluded that "this pernicious book is apparently a part of the political machinery which is being used by a political faction to deprive the colored people of the old Cotton States of all their political and civil rights."[13]

Accompanying the literary and judicial assaults on the Fourteenth and Fifteenth amendments were physical assaults against Black folk in the South and in cities in the North.[14] Lynching was one of the extralegal devices used to secure the disfranchisement of Black men. Ida B. Wells, a Black journalist from Memphis, Tennessee, and the woman who was to emerge as the chief architect of an international crusade against lynching, recounted the struggle of the Black man to exercise the franchise in her *Red Record* of 1895:

The government which had made the Negro a citizen found itself unable to protect him. It gave him the right to vote, but denied him the protection which would have maintained that right. Scourged from his home, hunted through the swamp, hung by midnight riders and openly murdered in the light of day, the Negro clung to his right of franchise with a heroism that would have wrung admiration from the hearts of savages. He believed that in the small white ballot there was a subtle something which stood for manhood as well as citizenship, and thousands of brave black men went to their graves exemplifying the one by dying for the other.[15]

The legal definition of a lynching is a murder committed by a mob of three or more persons. There are no accurate figures as to the number of lynch victims, and the estimates vary. James Elbert Cutler, who produced the first scholarly treatment on the subject in 1905, estimated that 3,337 human beings were lynched in the United States between 1882 and 1903.[16] According to a later study by the National Association for the Advancement of Colored People (NAACP) issued in 1929 and based upon only those killings acknowledged by white officials, 4,951 persons were lynched in the United States. Approximately 3,500 were Black, and 1,400 were white.[17] Wells placed the number of lynch victims at 10,000 before the turn of the century.[18]

The lynchings were savage affairs. Hundreds if not thousands of white people participated in the torture and killing of one or two individuals. Souvenirs in the form of body parts, pieces of rope, and clothing were often taken by members of the mob. Mary Church Terrell, founding president of the National Association of Colored Women (NACW), and the head of the Anti-Lynching Bureau of the National Afro-American Council, described lynching as "the aftermath of slavery. . . . It is impossible to comprehend the cause of the ferocity and barbarity which attend the average lynching-bee without taking into account the brutalizing effect of slavery upon the white people of the South."[19]

In combating this terror, Ida B. Wells and the Black women of the antilynching crusade made an important contribution to the emancipation of Southern womanhood from the particular ravages of a patriarchal culture embedded in racist dogma. For the fundamental rationale used to justify the lynching of Black men was their alleged rape of white women. In the words of one scholar:

> The myth of the black rapist reached pathological proportions at the turn of the century, in part because of its congruence with the exaggerated sexual tensions of a dying Victorianism. . . . No image so dramatically symbolized the most lurid of Victorian fantasies and fears as that of a violent sexual congress between a black man and a white woman. . . .
> . . . Rape and rumors of rape became a kind of acceptable folk pornography. . . . The experience and condition of the woman . . . were described in minute and progressively embellished detail: a public fantasy that implies a kind of group participation in the rape of the woman almost as cathartic as the subsequent lynching of the alleged attacker.[20]

Despite the correlation of lynching and rape in the public mind, only twenty-three percent of the *known* victims of lynch mobs between 1882 and 1946 were even accused of rape or attempted rape. Study after study has also shown that the vast majority of rapes are intraracial. In cases of interracial rapes it was Black women who were victimized, by an overwhelming number.

Nevertheless, so widespread was the correlation between lynching and rape in the public mind that even so enlightened a social reformer as Jane Addams accepted it, although she was an early and courageous supporter of the antilynching movement.[21] The editor of *Harper's Weekly* ranted against "social equality" between the races, and the "new negro crime." "The obvious reason why white people at the South look with distrust on highly educated negroes," he continued, "is because the latter are most likely to aim at social equality, and to lose the awe with which, in slavery times, black men had learned to regard the women of a superior race."[22]

Ida B. Wells and the Black women of the antilynching crusade insisted that the only effective challenge to lynching was one which disabused the Black man-as-rapist syndrome. In detailing one atrocity after another for forty years, Wells also suggested that some white women preferred the company of Black men and that Black women who were repeatedly raped by white men never knew the benefits of so-called Southern chivalry.

In defending the racial integrity of Black manhood, Wells simultaneously affirmed the virtue of Black womanhood and the independence of white womanhood. For the dialectics of the lynch mentality required the dehumanization of Black men (as rapists), Black women (as prostitutes), and white women (as property whose honor was to be avenged by the men who possessed them). Just as rape was used to justify the lynching of Black men, so the mythology of the Black woman's sexual promiscuity and aggression were the main ideological vehicles used to "explain" the appetite of white men for Black women. Typical of the racist imagery directed against Black women is this article by a well-to-do Southern white woman, writing on the race problem in a national magazine in 1904:

[D]egeneracy is apt to show most in the weaker individuals of any race; so negro women evidence more nearly the popular idea of total depravity than the men do. They are so nearly lacking in virtue that the color of a negro woman's skin is generally taken (and quite correctly) as a guarantee of her immorality. On the whole, I think they are the greatest menace possible to the moral life of any community where they live. And they are evidently the chief instruments of the degradation of the men of their race. . . . I sometimes read of virtuous negro women, hear of them, but the idea is absolutely inconceivable to me. . . . I cannot imagine such a creation as a virtuous black woman.[23]

It is out of the experience and from this point of view that the antilynching movement of Black women may also be understood as a movement against rape. The women used the only political forms and arguments available to them. They forged a movement that, for the first time in United States history, made rape a political issue.

It was not until the 1930s that white women in the South finally rose to attack the rape-lynching mythology. Under the leadership of a Texas woman, Jessie Daniel Ames, the Association of Southern Women for the Prevention of Lynching (ASWPL) was organized. For twelve years, thousands of these women, organized largely through the Methodist church, hammered home the fact that Black men were being lynched for reasons other than the raping of white women. These women also challenged the right of white men to hold possession of their person and honor.[24]

At the height of the lynch terror at the turn of the century, and precisely when the campaign for nullification of the Fifteenth Amendment had reached its most dangerous level, some of the leaders of the NAWSA compromised their founding principles of universal suffrage. Succumbing to racist pressures, they endorsed the idea of a more restrictive suffrage, adopted expedient arguments in defense of their position, and supported or acquiesced in the theory of state's rights. This was done in the belief that Southern whites could be more effectively won to the suffrage cause if their fears were assuaged. In reality, the dynamic of such a compromise was precisely to encourage the racist posture and the legitimacy of restricting the right of suffrage.

The 1903 national convention of NAWSA was held in New Orleans. Susan B. Anthony, Carrie Chapman Catt, Alice Stone Blackwell, Anna Howard Shaw, and many others signed a letter published in the *New Orleans Times-Democrat*, assuring their Southern supporters that NAWSA believed in the principle of state's rights, and that the race question was irrelevant to its purposes.[25] The NAWSA leadership had, in fact, endorsed the de facto disfranchisement of Black men despite its constitutional guarantee.

Black people, however, were by no means content to abandon the woman suffrage movement to the exigencies of racist pressures. From a practical point of view, few other causes could claim to unite so large a section of the white population as did woman suffrage. It was an authentic and progressive mass movement. Moreover, suffragists had a well-known abolitionist heritage, and their success now could advance the cause of Negro rights by affirming the Fifteenth Amendment and extending the suffrage. For a newly emerging civil-rights movement that was fighting a defensive, all-consuming battle for the survival of the race, an alliance with the woman suffrage movement represented one of the few tangible opportunities for potential success.

Black leaders appealed directly to the women. In an address before the NAWSA convention of 1912, W. E. B. Du Bois said:

The advocates of woman suffrage have continually been in great danger of asking the ballot not because they are citizens, but because they occupy a certain social position, are of a certain grade of intelligence, or are "white." Continually it has been said in America, "If Paupers and Negroes vote why not college-bred women of wealth and position?" The assumption is that such a woman has superior rights to have her interests represented in the nation and that Negroes and Paupers have few rights which society leaders are bound to respect. . . . Such argument is both false and dangerous, and while its phrasing may be effective at times it represents a climbing of one class on the misery of another.[26]

Du Bois's speech had considerable appeal, and it was published as a pamphlet by NAWSA. It was delivered as NAWSA itself, furbished with new leadership and energy, embarked upon a vigorous national campaign. Soliciting the Black man's vote in Northern states where the suffrage issue was on the ballot made the principled alliance a practical one as well.

Some months later Du Bois informed readers of the *Crisis* that he thought racism in the woman suffrage movement had been largely set back. There can be little doubt that many white women were persuaded that racism was contrary to their own best interests. By 1917 the NAWSA finally condemned lynching in a convention resolution. This represented a significant shift from the pro-racist line of the 1903 convention in New Orleans.[27]

"Let every black man and woman," Du Bois wrote in 1913, "fight for the new democracy which knows no race or sex."[28] The Black vote in favor of suffrage was a significant factor in several Northern and Western elections including California (1911), Pennsylvania (1915), and New York (1917).[29]

Black women were to be found among the activists in the organized suffrage movement. Outstanding among them were Mary Church Terrell, Ida B. Wells, Josephine St. Pierre Ruffin, Sarah Garnet, Margaret M. Washington, Ida R. Cummings, and Elizabeth L. Davis. The National Association of Colored Women, which had a membership of 50,000 by 1914, ardently supported the suffrage cause. For the Black women, the suffrage issue was always posed as a universal principle of citizenship.

Mary Church Terrell, a life-long member of NAWSA and the first Black woman to serve on a board of education anywhere in the United States (she was appointed to the Washington, D.C., Board of Education in 1894), was a frequent speaker at suffrage conventions. Her first such appearance was on February 18, 1898, at the Columbia Theater in Washington, on the fiftieth anniversary of the Seneca Falls, New York, woman's rights convention. Her speech was titled, "The Progress of Colored Women." She began this way:

Fifty years ago a meeting such as this, planned, conducted and addressed by women would have been an impossibility. Less than forty years ago, few sane men would have predicted that either a slave or one of his descendants would in this century at least address such an audience in the nation's capital at the invitation of women representing the highest, broadest, best type of womanhood, that can be found anywhere in the world. Thus to me this semi-centennial of the National American Woman Suffrage Association is a double jubilee, rejoicing as I do, not only in the prospective enfranchisement of my sex but in the emancipation of my race.[30]

Black women also formed suffrage leagues to fight for enforcement of the Fifteenth Amendment and the extension of suffrage to women. Sarah Garnet was founder of the Equal Suffrage League, an organization of colored people in the New York area committed to the struggle for equal rights. Mrs. Garnet was a public school teacher in the Williamsburg section of Brooklyn, the first Black woman to serve as the principal of an integrated public school (Grammar School 81 on East 17th Street in New York City), and the widow of the famed abolitionist leader Henry Highland Garnet. She was also superintendent of the Suf-

Suffrage
and
Lynching

frage Department of the NACW. The noted Black educator
Hallie Quinn Brown described her as "the most noted suffragist of our race."[31]

Josephine St. Pierre Ruffin organized the Woman's
Era Club of Boston before the turn of the century and
edited the club's newspaper called the *Woman's Era*.
Ida B. Wells, the Mississippi-born daughter of former
slaves, founded the Alpha Suffrage Club in Chicago in
1914 for the purpose of organizing women of the race to
wield greater influence in city politics, and for winning
universal suffrage regardless of racial, sexual, or class
distinctions.[32]

It was in their crusade against lynching, however, that
Black women made their most important and unique
contribution to the cause of woman suffrage. For lynching, as we have already suggested, was intimately tied to
the de facto nullification of the Fifteenth Amendment.
And it was Wells who designed and organized what was
to become an ultimately irresistible movement. To appreciate the dimension of her effort, consider first its origin.

The crucial event in the career of Ida Wells was the
lynching of three Black men in Memphis, Tennessee, on
March 9, 1892. Although she knew all the victims, one of
them, Thomas Moss, was a particularly close friend. A
series of racist provocations by white Memphis businessmen, who were trying to force the Black proprietors of a
local grocery store out of business, finally culminated in
the triple slayings.

At the time of the lynching, Wells owned and edited the
only Black newspaper in town, the *Memphis Free Speech*.
In the weeks following the lynching she wrote successive
editorials demanding that the murderers be arrested and
tried. When the white-owned newspapers responded by
alleging that Black men were lynched because they raped
white women, Ida B. Wells replied with an editorial coup
de grâce that almost cost her life. She wrote: "Nobody in
this section of the country believes the old thread bare lie
that Negro men rape white women. If Southern white
men are not careful, they will over-reach themselves and
public sentiment will have a reaction; a conclusion will
then be reached which will be very damaging to the moral
reputation of their women."[33]

Having intimated that white women could be sexually

attracted to Black men, Ida Wells now faced the full fury of the white press and the mob itself. Some of the more prominent white businessmen gathered at the Memphis Cotton Exchange Building six days after Wells's editorial was published to openly propose her lynching. Luckily, she was out of the state, attending a general conference of the African Methodist Episcopal Church in Philadelphia.

With her life so threatened, Wells dared not return to Memphis. The offices of the *Free Speech* were sacked, creditors took possession of what was left, "and the *Free Speech* was as if it had never been," Wells wrote from New York City five months later.[34]

It was from New York that Wells launched the anti-lynching movement. She took a position as a writer for the *New York Age*, edited by T. Thomas Fortune. The *Age* was considered the most influential Black newspaper of its time. Its editor had been the founder of the National Afro-American League in 1887, which had as one of its central concerns an attack upon "the universal and lamentable reign of lynch and mob law" in the South.[35] Indeed, some years later when the league was reorganized as the National Afro-American Council, Ida Wells was to serve as the head of its Anti-Lynching Bureau.

Wells's experience in Memphis had convinced her that lynching had nothing to do with the so-called Negro crime:

Like many another person who had read of lynching in the South, I had accepted the idea meant to be conveyed—that although lynching was irregular and contrary to law and order, unreasoning anger over the terrible crime of rape led to the lynching; that perhaps the brute deserved death anyhow and the mob was justified in taking his life.

But Thomas Moss, Calvin McDowell and Will Stewart had . . . committed no crime against white women. This is what opened my eyes to what lynching really was. An excuse to get rid of Negroes who were acquiring wealth and property and thus keep the race terrorized and "keep the nigger down."[36]

On the basis of this experience, Wells determined to reveal the exact details of all lynchings that came to her attention. She believed that the concrete circumstances surrounding each case would show that vast numbers of lynch victims had not even been accused of criminal activities but, on the contrary, had been murdered for economic and political reasons. She believed that in establishing lynching as a politically motivated act she could generate political opposition to it.

With the support and encouragement of T. Thomas Fortune, Wells published a long article in the *New York Age* on June 25, 1892, "in explanation of the editorial which the Memphis whites considered sufficiently infamous to justify the destruction of my paper. . . ."[37] Thereafter, Wells wrote two regular weekly columns for the *Age*, under her pen name Iola. Her column was called "Iola's Southern Field."

Wells's articles were greeted with nearly unanimous acclaim in the Black community. Typical were the comments of Frederick Douglass, who came from his home in Washington to see her. Douglass told Wells "what a revelation of existing conditions" in the South her stories had been to him.[38]

Requests for copies of the June 25 edition of the *Age* came from all parts of the country. Invitations to speak were also forthcoming. Black women especially responded to Ida B. Wells's appeals.

An ad hoc committee of 250 colored women organized a testimonial meeting to honor Wells's work. It was held at Lyric Hall in New York City on October 5, 1892, and was reputed to be "the greatest demonstration ever attempted by race women for one of their own number."[39] Present on the platform with Wells were several outstanding Black women, including Mrs. Gertrude Mossell of Philadelphia, Mrs. Josephine St. Pierre Ruffin of Boston, Mrs. Sarah Garnet of New York, and Dr. Susan McKinney of Brooklyn, one of the very few Black women physicians in the country.

"Iola" was emblazoned on a panel of electric lights across the back of the stage, and the programs for the evening were miniature copies of the now defunct *Free Speech*. A collection taken at the conclusion of the meeting netted a $500 contribution and Wells used the money to publish a longer version of her June article as a pamphlet. Titled *Southern Horrors, Lynch Law In All Its Phases*, the pamphlet began with an introduction by Frederick Douglass, whose endorsement assured the antilynching movement wide support among Black people. Douglass wrote:

You give us what you know and testify from actual knowledge. You have dealt with the facts with cool, painstaking fidelity and left those naked and uncontradicted facts to speak for themselves.

Brave woman! you have done your people and mine a service which can neither be weighed nor measured. If American conscience were only half alive, if the American church and clergy were only half christianized, if American moral sensibility were not hardened by persistent infliction of outrage and crime against colored people, a scream of horror, shame and indignation would rise to Heaven wherever your pamphlet shall be read.[40]

Following this effort, Wells determined to reach a larger international audience through participation in the World Columbian Exposition in Chicago in 1893. The World's Fair was in celebration of the 400th anniversary of the discovery of America. Hundreds of exhibits depicting the natural resources of the United States and the artistic and scientific achievements of the American people were on display at Jackson Park in Chicago. Thousands of people from the United States and Europe attended the fair, which was officially recognized and partly financed by the United States government. Despite repeated efforts by leaders of the Afro-American community, the board of directors of the Columbia Exposition denied facilities for an exhibit to show the progress of the colored people since Emancipation.

Ida B. Wells and Frederick Douglass raised the money to publish an eighty-one-page book called *The Reason Why The Colored American is not in the World's Columbian Exposition*. Wells partially wrote, compiled, edited, and published the book. Twenty thousand copies were distributed. Although written in English, the preface was in French and German as well.[41] Frederick Douglass wrote the introduction.

The book was a clearly reasoned, factual account of the position of the Negro people in the United States. It included a detailed description of the systematic disfranchisement of the Black people in the Southern states; a careful and thorough explanation of the Convict Lease System through which thousands of Black men had been forced back into virtual slavery; and a long essay by Wells

Suffrage and Lynching

entitled "Lynch Law," in which she rendered a detailed factual account of a dozen or more atrocities.

In addition, the well-known Black journalist I. Garland Penn wrote a substantial essay on "The Progress of the Afro-American Since Emancipation," recording achievements in art, music, literature, sculpture, journalism, and in the church, other professions, business, and industry. Presented too was a five-page listing of over seventy-five patented inventions granted by the United States government to colored persons between 1845 and 1891.

Finally, Ferdinand L. Barnett, a lawyer and the publisher of the first Black newspaper in Chicago, the *Chicago Conservator*, contributed a brief essay explaining "The Reason Why" the colored people had not been permitted to join the Columbian Exposition. Arguing that their participation would have shown Black people to be competent, intelligent, and creative human beings, Barnett contended that this would have been contrary to the still-dominant proslavery view of the Negro as indolent, shiftless, lazy, and sexually aggressive.

As a result of her leadership at the World's Fair, Wells was invited to the British Isles. The invitation came from Miss Catherine Impey, a Quaker activist and editor of an anti-imperialist Scottish journal, *Anti-Caste*, which defended the rights of the Indian people against British colonial rule.

Ida B. Wells engaged in two extensive speaking tours through Scotland and England. She raised large sums of money to wage her antilynching campaign in the United States, and she formed an English Anti-Lynching Committee. Very much in the tradition of the old abolitionist movement, Wells was able to tap into the highest echelons of British society for support. Early in 1894 she succeeded in putting together a delegation of esteemed British citizens who were to tour the American South. However

the South rose *en masse* against such a visit and the governors of the Southern States with one or two exceptions vehemently denounced the whole project. The statement of Governor O'Farrell of Virginia, himself an anti-lynching man, is typical of the Southern sentiment. "Things have come to a pretty pass in this country," he said in the *New York World,* "when we are to have a lot of

English moralists sticking their noses into our internal affairs. It is the quintessence of brass and impudence." The English committee never came to the country....[42]

Although the British delegation's visit was aborted, Wells's English tour nevertheless had an impact on the situation in the United States. *The Cyclopedic Review of Current History* of 1895 reported on her activities:

Mainly owing to the efforts of Ida Wells, the negro woman who was lately driven from Memphis, Tenn., there has been formed in England a league in sympathy with the persecuted southern negro. The Duke of Argyll, the Archbishop of Canterbury, and others, are its officers; there is a woman's auxiliary committee, of which Mrs. Humphrey is president. The treasury already contains £5,000. The league is to cooperate with a similar organization in America agitating against the lynching of southern negroes. The southern papers inveigh against this movement with a vehemence which recalls the old days previous to the war.[43]

Upon her return to the United States the *Philadelphia Press* published the full list of British members of the Anti-Lynching Committee, and it included fifteen members of Parliament, nine clergymen—among them the Right Reverend Edward White Benson, Archbishop of York and Primate of All England, and the editors of the *Manchester Guardian*, the *Bradford Observer, Contemporary Review, London Daily News, London Daily Chronicle*, and *London Daily Post*. Utilizing the prestigious positions of her English associates (especially the clergy), Wells was able to secure invitations to address predominantly white organizations in the United States that otherwise would have remained inaccessible to her.

The first petitions against lynching were introduced into the Congress of the United States by Henry Cabot Lodge in 1894. Mr. Lodge presented resolutions "adopted by sundry citizens of Boston and New England at a mass meeting held August 29, 1894 at Faneuil Hall, Boston, remonstrating against lynching, lawlessness and mob violence in the U.S."[44] Many more were to follow.

Shortly after the list of English sponsors of the Anti-Lynching Committee was published and circulated, some white Americans of comparable stature joined the committee, including Richard Watson Gilder of the *Century Magazine*, Samuel Gompers, President of the American

Federation of Labor, Miss Frances Willard of the Women's Christian Temperance Union, Archbishop Ireland, Dr. John Hall, W. Bourke Cochran, and Carl Schurz. For the first time also, a few prominent Southern whites responded to the antilynching effort and endorsed the committee's activities. These included Bishop David Lessums of the Protestant Episcopal diocese of Louisiana, Bishop Hugh Miller Thompson of Mississippi, and Bishop A. Van de Vyer of Virginia.

This was the beginning, then, of the organized opposition to lynching. Antilynching activities became the driving force behind the work of the National Afro-American Council and the National Association of Colored Women, and behind the formation of the NAACP.

The British opposition to lynching had a particularly salutary effect upon white civic leaders in Memphis. That city was among the largest exporters of cotton in the world, and Memphis businessmen depended upon the English textile industry for much of their trade. The businessmen feared that Ida B. Wells's disclosures, which were reported in the pages of every London newspaper, could have a decidedly negative influence on their commercial relations. As the historian David M. Tucker expressed it:

It was no surprise, then, that those Chamber of Commerce capitalists who owned the local white press felt compelled to reprint certain British reports of Miss Wells's lectures abroad in order to refute their charges against the Bluff City. The *Memphis Commercial Appeal* accused her of gross exaggeration and insisted that Memphis was really a decent place for blacks to live. But significantly, in this effort to repair the city's damaged reputation, newspaper editors at last condemned lynching unequivocally and even tried to make their position retroactive by insisting they had never approved of mob law.[45]

In any event, after Wells's British campaign there were no lynchings in Memphis for over twenty years.

The antilynching crusade was part of the emergence of a modern civil-rights movement in the United States. By the time of the First World War the antilynching movement had gathered considerable momentum. Demonstrations were held, presidential delegations organized, petitions circulated, lawsuits filed, appeals published, and congressional action sought. The first antilynching legislation was introduced in Congress in 1917 by Leonidas C. Dyer, a representative from Missouri.

Although the movement never succeeded in winning passage of federal antilynching legislation (the Dyer Bill passed the House and was filibustered to death in the Senate), it did force a national debate on the issue, and by the nineteen twenties the number of lynchings per year was reduced.[46] The antilynching movement began to undermine the credibility of racist appeals that Black men were rapists, killers, and savages. The movement helped to halt the drift toward nullification of the Fifteenth Amendment. These gains were essential for the passage of woman suffrage.

However badgered by political winds, the suffrage women in NAWSA were committed to winning a federal amendment. Under the presiding genius of Carrie Chapman Catt, an extraordinary campaign to secure congressional approval of the Nineteenth Amendment and its state-by-state ratification was started in 1913 with the presidency of Woodrow Wilson. Catt's "winning plan," as it was called, was a precise strategy with specific goals and dates, legislative details on individual men and their voting patterns in Congress and in every state. Catt and NAWSA also launched a drive to build an extensive network of state and local suffrage organizations.

Coincident with Wilson's inauguration, thousands of women massed in Washington, D.C., for an impressive march up Pennsylvania Avenue. Although attacked by a mob of white men, the women proceeded undaunted. At the same time, a smaller, more radical contingent of women led by Alice Paul began a campaign of picketing and civil disobedience at the White House. Women were arrested and many were brutalized in the Washington jails. Hunger strikes by the women to dramatize their cause resulted in forced feedings. NAWSA opposed Paul's tactics, but many historians concur in the opinion that these militant actions helped to spur the urgency of the moment.

Black women participated directly in all of these activities. Ida B. Wells marched in the 1913 parade and when Southern women objected to her participation, white women from Chicago brought her into the line of march, arm-in-arm. Mary Church Terrell, who lived in Washington, regularly picketed the White House. The first major national action by Delta Sigma Theta—today a predominantly Black, 100,000-member public service sorority—was joining the 1913 suffrage march under their own banner.

In March 1914 the Anthony amendment finally made its way out of the House and Senate committees where it had been stalled by Southern legislators for twenty-five years. It failed to achieve the two-thirds and three-fourths majorities required in the respective floor votes, but it won a majority in the House and lost a majority in the Senate by only one vote.

After an enormous campaign by NAWSA on a national level, congressional adoption was won four years later—in the House on January 10, 1918, and in the Senate on June 4, 1919. Presidential support and women's work—both volunteer and industrial—in the First World War all contributed toward making the suffrage victory possible.

NAWSA now redoubled its efforts for the legislative battles in the respective states where ratification required a three-fourths majority. After the final victory in August 1920, Carrie Chapman Catt summarized the meaning of their labor and the suffrage victory:

It is doubtful if any man, even among suffrage men, ever realized what the suffrage struggle came to mean before the end was allowed in America. How much of time and patience, how much work, energy and aspiration, how much faith, how much hope, how much despair went into it. It leaves its mark on one, such a struggle. It fills the days and rides the nights. Working, eating, drinking, sleeping it is there. Not all women in all the States of the Union were in the struggle. There were some women in every State of the Union who knew nothing about it. But most women in all the States were at least on the periphery of its effort and interest when they were not in the heart of it. To them all its success became a monumental thing.[47]

As the issue of woman suffrage was pressed to the fore, Southern advocates of racist subjugation perceived the dynamics of the situation clearly. In June 1919 a representative from Missouri made a last ditch, unsuccessful effort to change the wording of the amendment to read: "The right of *white* citizens to vote shall not be abridged on account of sex."[48] Senator Lee S. Overman of North Carolina, who had headed the Woman Suffrage Committee in the

Senate from 1911 until 1916 and thwarted prosuffrage efforts to get the amendment out of committee, addressed his colleagues six days after the submission of it to the states for ratification. He condemned it as a reaffirmation of the Fifteenth Amendment:

I wonder if this is appreciated throughout the South? This latter Amendment simply goes a step further than the Fifteenth Amendment. In addition to saying that the right of suffrage shall not be abridged by reason of race, color and previous condition of servitude the new Amendment adds the word "sex." The language is not identical, but it is evident that the Woman Suffrage resolution is a post-script to the former Amendment which we have always opposed in the South.[49]

In the final months of struggle to secure ratification of the federal Woman Suffrage Amendment, Frederick Douglass's words uttered fifty years before, that woman suffrage "depended upon the preliminary success of Negro suffrage," echoed with chilling accuracy. Those who sought to defeat woman suffrage determined to unite the Southern states in endorsing an opposition resolution. They required the endorsement of thirteen states to stop the amendment. In the end ten states opposed ratification of woman suffrage. They were Delaware, Florida, Georgia, Mississippi, Alabama, South Carolina, North Carolina, Maryland, Louisiana, and Virginia.

Symbolic of what the whole century of struggle had been about, the last battle for ratification was fought out in the former slaveholding state of Tennessee. After a bitter struggle in which the enfranchisement of Black people was a pivotal issue, the Tennessee legislature voted its approval of the Woman Suffrage Amendment on August 18, 1920.[50]

Tennessee was the only former slaveholding state to approve the Nineteenth Amendment. NAWSA, of course, conducted a skilled lobbying effort during the legislative battle. It is probable too that Ida B. Wells's antilynching crusade, which had so influenced the direction of Memphis politics in the intervening years, helped to lay the basis for this victory.

When woman suffrage was finally passed, Black women by the thousands went to register to vote. Within a few days literacy tests, civil-service type examinations, proof of birth, and a myriad of other devices were invented to prevent Black women from registering. In some instances Black women were arrested on trumped up charges charges of "perjury" when they sought to register. William Pickens, on the staff of the NAACP, wrote about the new betrayal and concluded with an appeal to the white women of the United States: "Every method has been employed against the colored man, up to 'red shirt,' and 'ku klux' campaigns. . . . In some districts a colored man seals his death warrant by even attempting to register. Nothing in the code of 'Southern Chivalry' will prevent similar treatment of colored women. Will the women of the United States who know something at least of disfranchisement tolerate such methods to prevent intelligent colored women from voting?"[51]

W. E. B. Du Bois hailed the victory of woman suffrage even as he wrote: "To think that we had to wait until 1920 for the Woman Suffrage. . . . Yet in this very fact lies hope for us: A civilization that required nineteen centuries to recognize the Rights of Women can confidently be expected some day to abolish the Color Line."[52]

The legal recognition of suffrage rights, however, was only the first infantile step on the long road to woman's emancipation. The two freedom movements remained locked in uneasy embrace well into the last half of the twentieth century.

4

On "The Damnation of Women": W. E. B. Du Bois
and a Theory for Woman's Emancipation

When I was eight years old my parents took me to a Christmas party at the home of W. E. B. Du Bois and Shirley Graham Du Bois. It was not the first time I had been there, but it is the first independent recollection I have of it. They lived in a two-story gray stone house at 31 Grace Court in Brooklyn. Their home was only a short distance from the East River. At the front of the house was a small wrought iron fence with a gate. I believe we walked down a few steps to the front door. Dr. Du Bois's study was to the right of the front door—a large carpeted room with windows facing the street, crowded with books, filing cabinets and, as I remember, papers and folders everywhere. Somewhere off to the left of the front door was a small alcove, and then straight ahead beyond it was the kitchen. To the left of the kitchen there was an outdoor courtyard or terrace, which was then covered with freshly fallen snow. Upstairs I remember a spacious living room, with its enormous windows and red floorlength drapes, a richly colored Chinese silk-screen on one wall, a finely crafted grand piano, and the tallest, most beautifully decorated Christmas tree I had ever seen. The room hummed with the sound of a large crowd. The Christmas party that year was for the children of Julius and Ethel Rosenberg. It was December 1952.

Dr. and Mrs. Du Bois were part of my childhood. I remember too that I was scrubbed and polished for these occasions, my hair done up in braids and ribbons, my beloved jeans and t-shirts discarded for an appropriate skirt and blouse. (I think I stubbornly refused my mother's attempts at dresses altogether.) The Du Boises left the United States to live in Ghana in 1961, when I was sixteen years old. My mother, father, and I drove them to the airport.

I loved Dr. Du Bois as only a child could love a revered elder. He told me stories which I thought he made up for me on the spot. He sang songs while I played the piano, and held his note for as long as it was necessary for me to find mine. He had a delicious laugh, and a mischievous sense of humor, and together we occasionally pulled little pranks, especially on Mrs. Du Bois. I don't remember the content of most of this. I remember what children most always remember, I think: the feelings—of warmth, delight, and laughter—with which he left me.

When I was a little older and he was in Accra and I was in Berkeley, I wrote to him relating stories about our civil-rights sit-ins and picket lines. I remember one phrase in one of his letters back: "Out of the mist of years," he wrote, "I thank you all."

So it was with considerable love and not a little trepidation that I approached the writing of the essay that follows. Against the backdrop of childhood memory, Du Bois's essays and stories flowed, and his presence assumed now a different stride and another voice. My writing allowed me to work through a piece of my growing up and confirm rather than rock the memory of feeling which the name Du Bois always evoked in me. For in his writing too, even in its thunder, there was that same quality of energy, that attention to humor and the little details of life that I had so cherished and honored.

W. E. Burghardt Du Bois, the founder of the modern Afro-American and African liberation movements, and the father of Pan-African socialism, was a scholar of extraordinary depth and scope. Historian, sociologist, anthropologist, essayist, poet, novelist, editor, and, above all, teacher, Du Bois began the scientific study of the Afro-American and African peoples in an era when predominant scientific and theological opinion held the Negro to be an inferior, if not subhuman, form. Du Bois was, therefore, a pivotal figure in the struggle for human rights and, consistent with this humanitarian impulse, he was strikingly advanced in his views on women. Indeed, a conspicuous theme in much of his work is the subjugation of women, especially Black women. Dr. Du Bois issued many intelligent appeals for their emancipation.

Du Bois's contribution to the struggle for woman's emancipation was threefold. He originated theoretical ideas on the nature of woman's oppression and liberation. He gave practical assistance and support to the woman suffrage movement. And he focused special attention on the particular suffering of Black women, as well as on their unique contributions to both racial and sexual liberation.

Du Bois's most important book from the point of view of its concern with woman's emancipation was *Darkwater*, published in 1920. In his essay "The Damnation of Women," he declared that "the uplift of woman is, next to the problem of the color line and the peace movement, our greatest modern cause."[1]

A striking feature of this essay was its affinity with Socialist thought. Du Bois appeared to have been particularly influenced by Charlotte Perkins Gilman, an early feminist scholar whose classic study, *Women and Economics*, was published in 1898. Du Bois described what he called the "unendurable paradox" of woman's position in society: "The world wants healthy babies and intelligent workers. Today we refuse to allow the combination and force thousands of intelligent workers to go childless at a horrible expenditure of moral force, or we damn them if they break our idiotic conventions. Only at the sacrifice of intelligence and the chance to do their best work can the majority of modern women bear children. This is the damnation of women."[2]

Du Bois proposed the following solution: "The future woman must have a life work and economic independence. She must have knowledge. She must have the right to motherhood at her own discretion."[3]

Observing the vast increase in the numbers of working women (between 1910 and 1920 the number of women in the work force doubled, increasing from 4 to 8 million), Du Bois noted that some men were demanding that these women return to home and children. He disagreed and instead hailed "the revolt of white women" which, he said, had now reached "splendid proportions." Du Bois continued: "We cannot abolish the new economic freedom of women. We cannot imprison women again in a home or require them all on pain of death to be nurses and housekeepers."[4]

Writing nearly sixty years ago, Du Bois expressed many of the modern themes of the feminist movement. He understood that only with the combination of economic independence and reproductive freedom could woman rise to a position of equality and dignity with man. Du Bois

*Du Bois
and Woman's
Emancipation*

saw too the implications of this for realizing the human
potential in relationships between men and women that
would no longer be sexually or economically exploitative.
Perceiving in the liberation of woman the true liberation
of man from the "freedom" to dehumanize and plunder
woman, Du Bois wrote: "The present mincing horror of a
free womanhood must pass if we are ever to be rid of the
bestiality of a free manhood; not by guarding the weak in
weakness do we gain strength, but by making weakness
free and strong."[5]

Exploring the further dimensions of woman's oppression, Du Bois noted that he could clearly recall four wom-
en from his childhood: "my mother, cousin Inez, Emma
and Ide Fuller. They represented the problem of the widow, the wife, the maiden and the outcast." He continued:
"They existed not for themselves, but for men; they were
named after men to whom they were related and not after
the fashion of their own souls. They were not beings, they
were relations and these relations were enfilmed with
mystery and secrecy."[6]

Du Bois's focus was on the particular damnation of
Black women, upon whom the "crushing weight of slavery fell." Raging against the legally sanctioned sexual
abuse of Black women under slavery, Du Bois wrote:

I shall forgive the white South much in its final judgment day: I
shall forgive its slavery, for slavery is a world-old habit; I shall forgive its fighting for a well-lost cause, and for remembering that
struggle with tender tears; I shall forgive its so-called "pride of
race," that passion of its hot blood, and even its dear old laugh-
able strutting and posing; but one thing I shall never forgive, neither in this world nor the world to come: its wanton and continued and persistent insulting of black womanhood which it
sought and seeks to prostitute to its lust.[7]

Apprehending one of the great ironies of slavery, Du
Bois asserted that because Black women had been forced
to labor in the fields and had suffered all the punishments
meted out to men, they had attained an equality with
Black men unknown to their white counterparts. "Our
women in black," Du Bois wrote, "had their freedom con-
temptuously thrust upon them." This history of abuse, Du
Bois continued, was both "fearful and glorious. . . . It has
birthed the haunting prostitute, the brawler, and the
beast of burden; but it has also given the world an efficient

womanhood, whose strength lies in its freedom and whose chastity was won in the teeth of temptation and not in prison and swaddling clothes." Having attained this freedom, this independence from men, Du Bois concluded, Black women were in a position to give leadership to the whole struggle for woman's emancipation and "have a vast influence on the thought and action of the land."[8]

In his essay, "The Damnation of Women," Du Bois combined the Socialist theory of Charlotte Perkins Gilman with his own analysis of the Black experience, and so projected a new theory that saw the potential emancipation of all women in the independence of Black women. The practical implications of this theoretical conclusion were the possibility of and necessity for an alliance between the two freedom movements, which would be mutually beneficial: "When, now," he wrote, "two of these movements—woman and color—combine in one, the combination has deep meaning."[9]

How deep a meaning was further explored by Du Bois in his memorable fable "The Princess of Hither Isles," also published in *Darkwater*. In this story a daring theme is presented. Du Bois evokes the commonality of oppression as the wellspring for the sexual and emotional attraction white women have toward Black men.

The Hither Isles were "flat and cold and swampy," wrote Du Bois, and the white princess sat upon her throne, "lonely and full weary of the monotone of life." She longed to journey to the Yonder Kingdom on the mountainside, "where the sun shone warm." So the princess was glad when the king of Yonder Kingdom approached her throne, and bid her accompany him as his wife. Still, she noticed that she did not love the colorless man and "could not love him," although she tried to feign pleasure and excitement at his arrival and proposal. As the princess sat upon her throne, trying to decide what course to pursue, a Black beggar passed by, far below her, making his way through the slime and cold of the swamp. The beggar turned his head upward and the princess saw him. She straightened on her throne and the beggar turned to look at her:

and she shivered forward on her silver seat; he looked upon her full and slow and suddenly she saw within that formless black

and burning face the same soft, glad and gleaming of utter understanding, seen so many times before. She saw the suffering of
endless years and endless love that softened it. She saw the burning passion of the sun and with it the cold, unbending duty-
deeds of upper air. All she had seen and dreamed of seeing in the
rising, blazing sun she saw now again, and with it myriads more
of human tenderness, of longing and of love.[10]

The princess went with the king of Yonder Kingdom. Always the king cast a shadow over her, and between her
and the Black beggar who followed far behind. Finally
they arrived at the mountain's "topmost peak," and the
king "bent to the bowels of the earth and bared its golden
entrails, —all green and gray and rusted."

The Black man "whirled his slim back against the glory
of the setting sun and stood somber in his grave majesty,
enhaloed, transfigured, outstretching his long arms, and
around all heaven glittered jewels in a cloth of gold."

The princess saw him, "moaned in mad amaze, then
with one wilful wrench she bared the white flowers of her
breast and snatching forth her own red heart held it with
one hand aloft while with the other she gathered her robe
and poised herself."

The king, now aware of the Black man's presence,
screamed: "It's a nigger. It's neither God nor man, but a
nigger!" Still, the princess stepped forward toward the
Black beggar and toward the distant shore behind him
where she could see the mighty empire of the Sun. The
king grabbed his sword and cried out: "Never! for such
were blasphemy and defilement and the making of all
evil." Then the king raised his sword and with all the
strength at his command he struck the "little white heart-
holding hand until it flew armless and disembodied up
through the sunlit air."

Du Bois ended his parable this way:

On yonder distant shore blazed the mighty empire of the Sun in
warm and blissful radiance, while on this side, in shadows cold
and dark, gloomed the Hither Isles and the hill that once was
golden, but now was green and slimy dross; all below was the sad
and moaning sea, while between Here and There flew the severed hand and dripped the bleeding heart.

Then up from the soul of the princess welled a cry of dark despair, —such a cry as only babe-raped mothers know and murdered loves. Poised on the crumbling edge of that great nothing-

ness the princess hung, hungering with her eyes and straining her fainting ears against the awful splendor of the sky.

Out from the slime and shadows groped the king, thundering: "Back—don't be a fool."

But down through the thin ether thrilled the still and throbbing warmth of heaven's sun, whispering "Leap."

And the princess leapt.[11]

The parable is complex. Du Bois captures the emptiness of white woman's class privilege. However, he also portrays the woman as a sexual object and, essentially, as a passive victim. On the other hand, in her very capacity for despair Du Bois has asserted her humanity, and her leap is seen as an act of decision rather than passivity. Still, in Du Bois's story, the woman remains ultimately dependent upon male provision and approval. There has been a shift in allegiance which Du Bois believes will help the woman, but there is not yet an autonomous and empowered woman.

Throughout the long campaign for woman suffrage, and afterwards as well, Du Bois sought to initiate a relationship with the organized woman's rights movement. He took many opportunities to forge a link between the two freedom struggles. The greatest obstacle to unity, in his opinion, was the racism in the woman's movement. He repeatedly warned suffrage leaders that their efforts to secure the franchise were being undercut by racism.

Nevertheless, Du Bois championed the woman's cause in the pages of the *Crisis*. He devoted two issues entirely to the question of suffrage, and wrote numerous editorials urging Black men to vote for it:

Why should the colored voter be interested in woman's suffrage? There are three cogent reasons. First, it is a great human question. Nothing human must be foreign, uninteresting or unimportant to colored citizens of the world. Whatever concerns half mankind concerns us. Secondly, any agitation, discussion or reopening of the problem of voting must inevitably be a discussion of the right of black folk to vote in America and Africa.

Finally votes for women mean votes for black women. . . . The enfranchisement of these women will not be a mere doubling of our vote and voice in the nation: it will tend to stronger and more normal political life, the rapid dethronement of the heeler and the grafter, and the making of politics a method of broadest philanthropic race betterment, rather than a disreputable means of private gain.[12]

*Du Bois
and Woman's
Emancipation*

When women marching for suffrage in Washington, D.C., in the spring of 1913 were attacked by mobs of white men, Du Bois wrote an editorial in the *Crisis* in which he excoriated the hoodlums, "many of them in uniform." He noted that Black men were not among the attackers. He ended his comment this way:

White men are on the firing line, and if they don't want white women for wives they will at least keep them for prostitutes. Beat them back, keep them down; flatter them, call them "visions of loveliness" and tell them that the place for woman is in the home, even if she hasn't got a home. If she is homely or poor or made the mistake of being born with brains, and begins to protest at the doll's house or the bawdy house, kick her and beat her and insult her until in terror she slinks back to her kennel or walks the midnight streets. Don't give in; don't give her power; don't give her a vote whatever you do. Keep the price of women down; make them weak and cheap.

Shall the time ever dawn in this land of the brave when a free white American citizen may not buy as many women as his purse permits? Perish the thought and Hail Columbia, happy land![13]

In April 1915, Harriet Stanton Blatch, daughter of Elizabeth Cady Stanton, cofounder of the modern woman's rights movement, wrote to Du Bois asking his sponsorship of a centennial committee planning a celebration of the 100th anniversary of Mrs. Stanton's birth. Du Bois responded promptly and affirmatively, saying, "I should regard it as an honor."[14]

Ten years later, Margaret Sanger, pioneer advocate of birth control, wrote to Du Bois asking him to send a message to be read at the Sixth International Neo-Malthusian and Birth Control Conference, "to either encourage us to continue our work, or to express your frank opinion of what we should do and how to do it." Du Bois sent the following statement:

Next to the abolition of war in modern civilization comes the regulation of birth by reason and common sense instead of by chance and ignorance. The solution for both of these problems of human advance is so perfectly clear and easily accomplished that it is only kept back by the stupidity of mankind, the utter refusal of even educated persons to face the problem frankly. While this is, in the highest degree, discouraging, it is on the other hand encouraging to know that only "light, more light" is needed and here as elsewhere we have simply to keep everlastingly at it to bring ultimate triumph.[15]

Du Bois concentrated his attention in defense of Black women. Three significant research projects under his tutelage at Atlanta University focused on the neglects and needs of Black women as well as on their special contributions to society in general and to the Black community in particular.[16]

Many of Du Bois's books, and especially his novels, portray the Black woman as a competent, independent human being. *The Quest of the Silver Fleece* is particularly striking in this regard. The story is set in and around a swamp in Toomsville, Alabama, in the post-Reconstruction period. The main figure in the story is a Black girl, Zora. The story is, in fact, a celebration of her birth as woman. In presenting her strength, courage, beauty, and intelligence Du Bois envisions the rebirth of a people.

Du Bois delivers his message through his fictional characters, dissecting both black-belt Alabama and the larger culture which created it. . . . The novel is in the genre of Frank Norris' wheat epics *(The Octopus* and *The Pit)* for Du Bois uses cotton as the great force which controls the black man's destiny. However, the lasting value of *The Quest of the Silver Fleece* is its expression of Negritude. The real "silver fleece" is not in the cotton fields, but in the souls of black folk.[17]

However well he knew the souls of Black folk, Du Bois also knew something of the lives of white folk, and especially of white men and their treatment of women. Du Bois illustrates the relationship between racism and male supremacy as he depicts the ways in which the wives of the wealthy planters and financiers are treated as nonpersons to be seduced, laced with pretty things, and manipulated if they possessed either wealth or influence.

The only white person in the novel with any redeeming qualities is a New England schoolteacher, Sarah Smith. Du Bois portrays her as a truly heroic figure, battling with uncompromising determination to maintain a school for Black children.

Although designed in the genre of nineteenth-century romanticism, Du Bois abandoned the sexual hypocrisy of the Victorian mode in his novel. Through his portrayal of Zora, especially, we are able to visualize a warm, vital, ex-

Du Bois and Woman's Emancipation

plicitly sensual woman. In its sensuality, the novel introduced a literary style in Black writing developed by Jean
Tommer in his novel, *Cane,* published more than a decade
later.

In the pages of the *Crisis,* Du Bois championed the
cause of the Black woman. When she was abused, he ex-
posed it. Typical was his scathing report of the lynching of
a Black woman and her sixteen-year-old son in Oklahoma
in the summer of 1911, after both were accused of killing
the sheriff. A year later he excoriated the lynching in Pine-
hurst, Georgia, of another Black woman, Anne Bostwick—
a sixty-year-old servant accused of killing her employer's
wife. Likewise, Du Bois denounced the state of Virginia
and questioned the Christianity of its citizens for permitting the execution of a sixteen-year-old Black youngster
named Virginia Christian, charged with the murder of a
woman for whom she was a servant.[18]

Du Bois had a section of the *Crisis* called "Men of the
Month" in which he provided brief notes on race leaders.
Despite the subject heading, women were often included
in Du Bois's summary of notable personalities. Typical
was his report of the appointment of Coralie F. Cook to the
Board of Education in Washington, D.C.; or his mention of
Mrs. Ella E. Ryan of Tacoma, Washington, who was the
Black editor of the *Forum,* a newspaper which was read
almost entirely by white people, but which was very
strong on questions of segregation and racism; or the tribute to the Black educator, Hallie Quinn Brown: "Of all the
present forces among colored women, she is perhaps the
strongest and most far-reaching."[19]

The significance of Du Bois's consciousness of the so-
called woman question is twofold. First, he sees that part
of both the racist and antifeminist offensive that characterizes so much of American history is the effort to divide
Black and white people from each other, through the use
of sexual myths and stereotypes. For example, Black
women are depicted as castrating, emasculating, and aggressive matriarchs. Black men are alleged to be more sex-
ist than white men, and more given to rape, especially to
the rape of white women. The oppression of race is frequently alleged to be greater and more devastating than
the oppression of sex, as if a scorecard of human suffering was an appropriate comparative measure.

Du Bois's work illuminates the facade behind each of these divisions. He allows us to view the deep connection between racism and male supremacy—twin ideologies, as it were, of elitist dogma. He suggests the ways in which the two have intersected to sustain and reinforce our respective subjugation. Consequently, Du Bois appreciated the extent to which our liberations were mutually dependent upon one another, bound together by historical destiny. His work remains essential for contemporary readers.

Second, Du Bois himself is an example of a male figure who overcame centuries of male supremacist doctrine. That he was Black and did this is, of course, significant. Frederick Douglass was Black and a former slave, and he also embraced the woman's cause with a deep and abiding passion.

There are no comparable examples of white men in the United States who have distinguished themselves in this way, on this question. Du Bois and Douglass, however, were not alone among the Black men of their time in their appeal for the humanization of woman. As a result of the special oppression of Black women under slavery, an appreciation of the oppression of women forms an important part of the Black experience in the United States.

Still, as advanced as Du Bois's thinking was, he neglected an essential point, namely, that the subjugation of woman is the oldest form of human oppression, with origins that date back to several thousand years before Christ. It was, in essence, the first class division in society, for woman's oppression is rooted in the fact that she was made the property of man and reduced in a literal sense for centuries to the status of a slave. The legacy of this property relationship is the defining feature of woman's experience. It is embedded in law, theology, work, and in assumptions about marriage, the family, sexuality, and procreative capacity. Woman's emancipation will be the longest in coming because her oppression has been longest in the making.

That Black people, as a people, have been the most consistent, conscious, and dedicated adherents of woman's cause in the United States speaks to the commonality of the oppression. For this reason too, the emancipation of women of color will be the most complex and the most difficult, for she has been the property of white men in the double sense of being both woman/slave and chattel/slave, and oppressed by Black men under the male supremacist structure that has ultimately prevailed in the Black community as well.

Although Du Bois omitted direct and clear reference to the origin of woman's oppression in the ownership of private property, his socialist affinity, Black identity, and theoretical and practical work provide us with a primary vision of woman's emancipation.

5

Quest for Dignity: Black Women in the Professions, 1865 — 1900

While pursuing my master's degree at San Jose State in the mid-seventies, I enrolled in a graduate seminar, "Afro-American History: The Modern Era." I was the only white person in the class. The instructor was a powerful, provocative, and intensely rigorous Black woman. Dr. Gloria Alibaruho demanded excellence from her students and frequently got it. She was, in fact, one of the best teachers I have ever had. I read every assignment with acute attention and labored over every paper. In addition to the rigor which our professor rightfully pursued, I was nervous lest I "make a mistake"—which meant not so much a factual error as a racist one. I soon calmed down. It was all right to make a mistake. I started to learn. I engaged the material, felt the process of listening, of hearing new lines of argument and thought, people working through ideas in platforms, petitions, essays, and poems. History became a matter of experience and survival; and politics became the drama of history, deeply and irrevocably personal. It was in this class that I met Mrs. Carter, and it was her experience that ultimately suggested this essay on the history of Black women in the professions.

Mary Carter was born and raised in Alabama, the daughter of sharecroppers. She had worked the fields picking cotton since she was a child. She worked her way through nursing school, married, and eventually settled in California. Mrs. Carter had several children who were mostly grown, and she worked nights on the nursing staff at Stanford University's medical center. Now she was working toward her master's degree, and enjoying the opportunity of taking a free range of subjects in school. She took whatever she was interested in, and her interests were very wide indeed.

I thought Mrs. Carter was a beautiful woman. Yet, in thinking about how to describe her beauty for someone reading this, I am pressed to find the right juxtaposition of words. For however dark and radiant and soft her face, it also had about it an angularity and wisdom, a defiance and depth, the combination of which left me awed. Her voice was Southern, and she spoke with song in resonant, clarion tones.

We bonded first out of the need for mutual assistance in that graduate seminar. I had research skills and access to books and notes. Later too, I was helpful to her because I knew the university's administrative and institutional requirements. Mrs. Carter had patience and calm, scientific knowledge and an acute understanding of the world accumulated through her life and her educational and community experiences. We laughed a lot about the initial anxieties we both had had about our class. I think it was a great relief to each of us to share that admission with the other. However brief our rushed encounters during that semester, we worked hard and well together.

I finished my degree about a year and a half before Mrs. Carter. I began teaching. To my astonishment she enrolled in my class on "Afro-American Women in History." Her presence was very important to me because by it she acknowledged her belief that I could do this work in ways that were meaningful to her. A few months later she asked me to serve on the committee for her master's degree examination in Afro-American Studies.

Mrs. Carter had prepared for that exam with great care. She had read volumes on African and Afro-American history, literature, and culture. She was nervous, of course, before the exam; but she was also confident that she would pass. I knew this because she came early on the day of her exam, accompanied by her oldest son, who was dressed in formal clothes. He arrived with a camera in hand and sheer pleasure across his face. Mrs. Carter also brought an elaborate array of food and drink, home baked and beautifully displayed. We were all to share in her celebration afterwards.

The exam began with some preliminary questions, and then proceeded along a traditional academic line: would Mrs. Carter comment on the significance of this writer, on that school of thought, on someone's interpretation of such and such an event, and so on. Mrs. Carter proceeded well through this familiar territory. Then, one member of the committee asked her what she thought about so-and-so's interpretation of slavery. (I no longer remember which book, but it had something to do with the debate among *historians about the quality of slave life and the degree of slave resistance.)*

I cannot quote Mrs. Carter's exact words, but the substance of what she said was that she had given this matter a lot of thought; she herself had worked the fields since she was very little and she'd watched her parents, neighbors, and relatives, too. It's hard, hard work, Mrs. Carter said, exhausting work. Now, she continued, what had caught her attention in this book was what the author had reported about the slaves' diet. It was an insufficient diet, lacking protein and Vitamin B, and. . . . She went on for a while as her medical experience ticked off the deficiencies. Then, finishing her point, she concluded, "I don't know how a slave would manage to think on that kind of a diet and with that kind of work, and figure out that there was such a thing as freedom and what it was and how to get it. But we did," she said. "We did."

Mrs. Carter passed her exam and was awarded the master's degree in Afro-American Studies. Her son took many pictures, and we ate a fine meal.

Sometime in the course of our relationship, I learned that Mrs. Carter was the first Black woman ever hired as a nurse by Stanford University's medical center—in 1959. Although I knew of the hierarchical structure of the medical world, I had assumed that nursing was a profession open to women. It was from Mrs. Carter that I learned about the intensity of the discrimination against Black women. This experience directed me toward a more thorough inquiry into the history of Black women in the professions. "Quest for Dignity" was the result. It was inspired by my friendship with Mary Carter, and I respectfully and affectionately dedicate it to her.

O N September 22, 1891, a small notice appeared on the front page of the *New York Times* announcing the certification of "A Colored Female Doctor." The one-paragraph story, originating in Tuskegee, Alabama, read:

Mrs. Halle T. Dillon, M.D. (colored) daughter of Bishop B. T. Tanner, is not only the first colored female physician, but the first woman of any race to pass the Alabama State Medical Examination. It was a written examination and an unusually severe one,

occupying ten days. Dr. Dillon, after passing with a high average,
now occupies the position of resident physician at Tuskegee
Institute.

While Dr. Dillon was not the first Black woman physician in the United States, the *Time*'s front-page coverage
was understandable, considering the general ideological
and political bent of the white, male medical world. That
Black women penetrated the profession at all was one of
the better accomplishments of modern medicine in the
nineteenth century.

1   The first Bachelor of Arts degree was not awarded to a
Black woman until 1862, when Mary Jane Patterson
(1840—1894) was graduated from Oberlin College. Anna
Julia Cooper, principal of the Colored High School in
Washington, D.C., and herself an Oberlin graduate, conducted a survey early in 1890 to discover the number of
Black women who had graduated from universities
known to admit female students. Cooper reported that
only thirty Black women had completed the B.A. degree
in the entire history of these universities.[1] Cooper also
noted that in June 1890 a colored woman was graduated
from Cornell University with the first Bachelor of Science
degree.

A 1910 study revealed that 107 "non-Negro colleges"
had graduated 114 Negro women in their collective histories, with the largest number (66) coming from Oberlin. Of
the Negro colleges, Howard and Fisk led the way, having
graduated 514 women by 1910.[2]

Prior to the Civil War, the majority of Black people with
any degree of formal education, men and women, went
into teaching. There were a few Black physicians and dentists, but, as Kelly Miller of Howard University observed:
"the colored physician had appeared as an occasional or
exceptional individual" and did not constitute a professional class. Following the war, colleges and universities
"were planted in all parts of the South for the sake of preparing leaders for the newly emancipated race. Several
medical schools were established in connection with
these institutions."[3]

Howard University's medical school opened its doors
in 1868 with eight students. Meharry Medical College was

organized in 1876 as part of Central Tennessee College in Nashville. Shaw University in Raleigh, North Carolina, set up the Leonard Medical School in 1880, and New Orleans University created the Flint Medical College in 1889.

Despite great effort, only Meharry and Howard were to survive. In 1910 Abraham Flexner published his now-famous report on *Medical Education in the United States and Canada,* under the auspices of the Carnegie Foundation. This report strongly influenced the setting of standards for medical colleges and its racist content had a heavy impact on the Negro schools. Chapter fourteen was devoted to a discussion of the "Medical Education of the Negro." Flexner conceded that it was appropriate to have Negro doctors, as long as their practice was limited to Negro patients; however, he described most of the Negro colleges as "ineffectual . . . wasting small sums annually and sending out undisciplined men, whose lack of real training is covered up by the imposing M.D. degree." Only Meharry and Howard, he thought, were worth saving.[4]

Small numbers of Black women did graduate from medical and law schools prior to the turn of the century. Of the 3,855 Black doctors in the United States in 1920, however, less than one-half of one percent were women; and eighty-three percent of the Black doctors were graduates of either Howard or Meharry, reflecting the racist quota systems practiced throughout the United States.[5] While Black people were generally excluded from white institutions, a few women were able to gain admission to the female medical colleges, and sometimes even to male-run medical colleges.

For those pursuing a medical career, however, receiving a degree was only the beginning. Internships in established hospitals were prerequisite to certification by the 1880s, and generally were required even before that. These were almost impossible to obtain if you were Black and/or a woman. As one medical historian explained: "Practically all the male dominated institutions barred women from their internship programs. One female medical school graduate became so desperate in 1857 that she volunteered to enter Boston Hospital as a patient in order to gain clinical training, but to no avail."[6]

In addition, Black women faced racial discrimination which sometimes barred them even from women's hospitals. The NAACP reported in 1915, for example, that "the well known case of Isabella Vandervall who led her class during her whole course at the Women's Hospital, New York City, illustrates this situation. She was appointed intern at the Syracuse Hospital for Women and Children and then the hospital peremptorily refused to fulfill its contract when they discovered that she was of Negro descent."[7]

Women placed priority on establishing their own colleges and hospitals, which remained the single most important source of female internship programs until well into the twentieth century. In the Afro-American community as well, efforts were made to set up training schools and hospitals for nurses and doctors, with significant success.

Additionally, the established professional associations barred women and Black people from membership. Their fates were linked together in much the same way as they were in the battle for suffrage. Writing on the struggle of women to gain admission to American medical societies, one historian observed:

The opponents of woman's rights related the situation of women to that of the Negro. At the same time as he argued against the entrance of women into the profession, for instance [one doctor] attacked the Negro's right to advance. [Another] also commented on the rights of Negroes to enter the profession, when he said: "We must look the thing in the face, black as it may be. What has the Negro done to entitle him to recognition by medical societies?" he asked. "Has he shown any capability for scientific attainment? Has he contributed anything to medical science?" The answer was simple: "He has not. He is merely pushed forward by politicians whom I hate and despise." The implications of this line of argument seemed to be that if women were admitted to the profession, Negroes would be the next logical step, and they were even more objectionable than women.[8]

Women finally gained admission to the American Medical Association in 1915, but maintained their own professional association as well, as an appropriate counterforce to the male supremacist structure of the AMA. Black physicians were barred from many local chapters of the AMA (especially in the South) under the guise of "home rule" authority, until the late 1960s. Repeated efforts to get the AMA to change its national constitution to affirm antiracist principles failed. It was not until the 1950 edition of the American Medical Directory (published by the AMA) that the designation "colored" was dropped after the names of Negro doctors.

In response to these realities, Black professionals formed their own associations shortly after the turn of the century. In its constitutional preamble the National Medical Association defined its purpose: "Conceived in no spirit of racial exclusiveness, fostering no ethnic antagonism, but born of the exigencies of the American environment, the National Medical Association has for its object the banding together for mutual co-operation and helpfulness, the men and women of African descent who are legally and honorably engaged in the practice of the cognate professions of Medicine, Surgery, Pharmacy and Dentistry."[9]

Moreover, the white intelligentsia in general and the medical profession in particular served as a bulwark for the perpetuation of racist and male supremacist ideology. Cloaked in the aura of scientific authenticity "the physician remained the chief source of information for comparative race analysis." According to one authority, "the belief in the Negro's extinction [as a consequence of inferiority] became one of the most pervasive ideas in American medical and anthropological thought during the late 19th century." Typical of the arguments were that

the Negro brain, some one thousand years "behind that of the white man's brain in its evolutionary data," existed within a visceral and organic structure that was physiologically juxtaposed to its intellectual capacity. The Negro's "moral delinquencies," along with elements of "bestiality and gratification," were demonstrations of the close relationship of the race to his "animal and sub-human ancestors." Confined within narrow physical functions, the Negro's nearness to a superior race merely accelerated his "innate tendency to sex appetite."[10]

Attitudes toward women were hardly more enlightened. Representative of the barrage of antifeminist literature in the late nineteenth century was the article by William A. Hammond, a leading Virginia doctor specializing in neurology and neuropsychology, which appeared in the *North American Review* in August 1883. Briefly summarized, Dr. Hammond argued that a man's brain was on the average five ounces heavier than a woman's and that the cerebral structure of the brain in each sex was consequently different, the proportion of gray matter at the frontal lobes being distributed differently in man and woman. Distinctions in brain size and structure confirmed Dr. Hammond's opinion that men were of a higher order of intelligence than women. The female brain, Hammond concluded, "is a brain from which emotion rather than intellect is evolved. Very few women are capable of an intense degree of abstract thought, no matter how much education they have received. The female brain, besides being emotional is, like that of the quadramana, an imitative brain. It is not capable of originating thought, though it copies well."[11]

Black women, allegedly approaching extinction and possessing the mental capacity of an anthropoid ape, encountered enormous obstacles as they sought to enter the professional world. Indeed, the combination of racial and sexual oppression forced the vast majority of Black women into the lowest paying and most menial labor. In 1910, nearly 95 percent of the Black women who were employed labored as agricultural and domestic workers. Only 3.5 percent were in factory work and an even smaller 1.5 percent were professionals, mainly teachers.[12]

I devoted this chapter exclusively to the achievements of Black women in the professional world because the discrimination against them was so intense that their names were frequently erased from historical records which otherwise noted the work of Black men or white women. The act of naming in this case meant literally finding the names of these Black women whose careers are noted in the pages that follow; and even after names were found, biographical details were sometimes still impossible to come by.

The *Journal of the American Medical Association* has had two articles in its history on Black physicians, one in 1942 and one in 1969. Neither contained any references to women. Standard works on the history of women in medicine mention Black women parenthetically and even the well-researched study of the *History of the Negro in Medicine* has only brief and fragmentary mention of the women.

My chief sources of information were those Afro-American women who recounted their experiences in their own books and magazines and in the journals of the Black professional associations. The real stories will begin to come, however, as descendant families of these women are located and their individual histories reconstructed.

2   The first Black woman to complete a medical course at an American university was Sarah Mapps Douglass (1806 — 1882). One of the founding members of the Philadelphia Female Anti-Slavery Society, Douglass was in charge of the girls' department of the Institute for Colored Youth in that city. She attended the Ladies' Institute of the Pennsylvania Medical University for three years, completing her studies in 1858. She then introduced scientific subjects, including physiology, into the curriculum of the girls' department, believing that the education of female children should not be limited to domestic and household skills.[13]

Another important figure in the abolitionist movement was Sarah Parker Remond (1826 — c.1887). A member of the Boston Female Anti-Slavery Society, she emigrated to Italy at the end of the Civil War to escape the indignities of race prejudice in the United States. She attended medical school in Florence, and received her degree in 1871, at the age of fifty-six. Mrs. Elizabeth Buffum Chace, a Quaker and friend of abolition, visited Florence in 1873. Her memoirs record an encounter with Dr. Remond, whom she described as a "remarkable woman." She continued, "By her indomitable energy and perseverance she has won a fine position in Florence as a physician and also socially." She quoted Dr. Remond as saying that Americans had attempted to use their influence to prevent her success "by bringing their hateful prejudices" to Italy.[14]

Rebecca Lee was the first Black woman doctor in the United States. She was graduated from the New England Female Medical College in 1864 and established a successful practice in Richmond, Virginia, after the Civil War. Her graduation, however, appears to have been clouded by race considerations. The faculty notes on Dr. Lee record that "*some* of us have hesitated very seriously in recommending her . . . and do only out of deference to what we understand to be the wishes of the Trustees and the present state of public feeling."[15] No other Black women were ever admitted to the college, which ceased to exist in 1874.

Dr. Rebecca Cole (1846 – 1922), the second Black woman to receive a medical degree in the United States, was a member of the class of 1867 at the Woman's Medical College in Philadelphia. Dr. Cole spent the Reconstruction years in Columbia, South Carolina. Upon her return to Philadelphia she worked with Dr. Charlotte Abby in establishing a Woman's Directory, which gave medical and legal aid to women. She was superintendent for several years of the Government House in Washington, D.C., for children and old women. In all, she practiced about fifty years.

A few Black women succeeded in graduating from white male medical schools. A more significant number were early graduates of the Woman's Medical College in Philadelphia, which apparently had a strong policy of admitting minority women in its earlier years.[16] Among the Black graduates was Dr. Caroline V. Still Anderson (1848 – 1919), the daughter of William and Letetia Still, famed abolitionist leaders and founders of the Underground Railroad and Vigilance Committee in Philadelphia. After her graduation from Woman's College, Dr. Anderson was at first refused admission to the New England Hospital for Women and Children on account of her race, but was later admitted as an intern. She returned to Philadelphia at the end of her internship, and established a dispensary and clinic at the Berean Presbyterian Church on South College Avenue. Her husband, the Reverend Matthew Anderson, was pastor of the church. Dr. Anderson was the founder of the Philadelphia YWCA for colored women, and a supporter of the temperance movement. She maintained her church clinic for nearly forty years.

Black women were the first women of any race to practice medicine in four Southern states. Three of them were graduates of the Woman's Medical College in Philadelphia. In most states prior to 1885, in order to register as a physician one had only to be endorsed by four practicing doctors. Gradually, with the professionalization and specialization so prevalent at the turn of the century, state licensing was required.

As already noted, Dr. Halle Tanner Dillon became the

first woman licensed to practice in Alabama. Dr. Verina Morton-Jones was the first woman licensed to practice in Mississippi, and Matilda A. Evans was the first woman licensed to practice in South Carolina. Dr. Sara G. Jones, a graduate of Howard Medical College in 1893, became the first woman of any race to pass the Board of Medical Examiners in Virginia.

Although the white male establishment was notoriously hostile to female practitioners, Black men were generally supportive and encouraging of women entering the medical profession. Dr. Monroe A. Majors, writing on the triumphs and activities of Negro women in 1893, paid tribute to his sisters in the medical profession, noting in general that "the criterion for Negro civilization is the intelligence, purity and high motives of its women."[17] The preamble of the NMA constitution included women as co-equals in its mission, and women were officers in the NMA. For example, Dr. Georgia R. Dwelle, a graduate of Meharry who began her practice in Atlanta, Georgia, in 1906, was vice-president of the NMA shortly after its founding, and Dr. Matilda Evans served as South Carolina vice-president of the NMA late in the twenties. The NMA's attention to the achievements of Black women continues to the present day.[18]

The majority of Black women were graduates of either Meharry or Howard because racial discrimination prevented their large-scale admission elsewhere. But, unlike many of their white female counterparts who faced severe sex discrimination in seeking employment in predominantly white institutions, several Black women were recruited as resident physicians in Negro colleges. Dr. Dillon was at Tuskegee from 1891 to 1894; Dr. S. Maria Steward (who graduated from medical school under her maiden name, Susan M. Smith, and practiced in New York City as Susan McKinney, assuming the name of her first husband) was at Wilberforce from 1897 until her death in 1918. Dr. Julia R. Hall served as resident physician at Miner Hall, Howard University, and Dr. Ionia R. Whipper was resident physician at Collegiate Institute in West Virginia and later at Tuskegee.

Halle Dillon's duties as resident physician at Tuskegee were extensive and typical of the demands placed upon resident physicians. She was responsible for the care of

Afro-American Women Physicians Graduated from Medical Schools in the United States (1864 – 1900)

New England Female Medical College		Anna W. McCormick	1883
		Mary L. Wooster	1883
Rebecca Lee	1864	Kate D. Barstow	1884
Woman's Medical College (Philadelphia)		Katherine F. Beatty	1884
		Mary E. Hartwell	1884
Rebecca Cole	1867	Mary Ellis Morrison	1886
Caroline V. Still Anderson	1878	Minnie C. T. Love	1887
Juana B. Drummond	1888	Marian Pyles	1888
Verina Morton-Jones	1888	Julia E. Smith	1889
Matilda A. Evans	?	Susan J. Squire	1889
Verena Harris	1889	Julia R. Hall	1892
Halle Tanner Dillon	1891	Sarah G. Jones	1893
Alice Woodby McKane	1892	May D. Baker	1896
M. E. Thompson Coppin	1900	Mary L. Brown	1897
New York Medical College for Women		Eunice Foster	1897
		Ameila F. Foy	1897
Susan M. Smith (McKinney)	1870	Lucy D. Moten	1897
Syracuse University		Elizabeth B. Muncey	1897
Sarah Logan Fraser	1876	Elizabeth Hampson	1898
University of Michigan		Mildred E. Gibbs	1900
Sophia B. Jones	1885	Harriet E. Riggs	1900
Tufts Medical College (before 1920)		*Meharry Medical College*	
Ruth Esterling		Oceola C. Queen	1891
Josefa Zaratt		Georgia E. L. Washington Patton	1893
Dorothy Boulding		Annie D. Gregg	1893
Jeannette Banks		Lucinda Davis Key	1894
Howard University		Otha D. Porter	1894
Mary D. Sparkman	1872	Val Do Turner	1894
Mary A. Parson	1874	Francis W. Puryear	1895
Frances S. Hillyer	1877	Fannie M. Kneeland	1898
Grace Roberts	1877	Mary Susan S. Moore	1898
Eunice P. Shadd	1877	Hattie L. Hadley	1898
Caroline A. Burghardt	1878	Annie B. Marsh	1899
Nannie W. Stafford	1878	Carrie L. Wilson	1899
Mary Ester Hart	1880	Lucille F. Miller Weathers	1900
Juliet Gambill Shearer	1882	J. Lucian Carwins	1900

Sources: Journal of the National Medical Association 60 (March 1968): 152 – 55; Herbert M. Morais, *History of the Negro in Medicine* (Washington, D.C.: Association for the Study of Afro-American Life and History, 1967); Monroe A. Majors, *Noted Negro Women: Their Triumphs and Activities* (1893; reprint ed., Freeport, N.Y.: Books for Libraries Press, 1971); Hallie Quinn Brown, *Homespun Heroines and Other Women of Distinction* (1926; reprint ed., Freeport, N.Y.: Books for Libraries Press, 1971); Sara W. Brown, M.D., "Colored Women Physicians," *Southern Workman* 52 (1923): 580 – 93; and *Who's Who in Colored America* (published annually beginning in 1927).
Note: This listing is probably complete only for Howard and Meharry graduates.

450 students, as well as thirty officers, teachers, and their families. She was also expected to make her own medicines, as Tuskegee could not afford to purchase already processed drugs. Beyond these duties, she taught one or two classes each term. Her salary was $600 a year, with board for twelve months, and a one month's vacation.[19]

Black women also served in high capacities in all-Negro hospitals which serviced the Black community. Dr. Sarah H. Fitzbutler was superintendent of the Auxiliary Hospital of the Louisville National Medical College from 1901, until it was forced to close in 1911 as a result of the Flexner Report. And Dr. Lillian Atkins Clark served as the chief resident at Douglass Hospital in Philadelphia from 1924 to 1926. Other Black women were regular staff physicians at Provident Hospital in Chicago, Freedmen's Hospital in Washington, D.C., and Douglass Hospital.

The main energies of Black doctors went into providing health care for the Black community. This took two forms: first, the establishment of Black-run hospitals, dispensaries, clinics, and training schools to service the community and provide internships for graduating nurses and doctors; and, second, massive educational campaigns on hygienic and health issues, especially against the ravages of tuberculosis. The thrust toward preventive medicine was particularly extensive in rural areas of the South, and was part of the National Negro Health Week annual campaigns organized by the NMA and supported by the NAACP, the Urban League, and the National Association of Colored Women.[20] Black women made special contributions to these and related efforts through their work in the NACW, and by virtue of their historic connection to the struggle for education. A significant number of the women specialized in obstetrics and gynecology, and/or pediatrics.

Dr. M. Fitzbutler Waring (daughter of Dr. Sarah H. Fitzbutler) was chairperson of the Department of Health and Hygiene for the NACW for more than fifteen years, beginning in 1911, and president of the NACW's Necessity Day Club Nursery in Chicago. Dr. Verina Morton-Jones was the head worker at the Lincoln Settlement House in Brooklyn, New York, director of the NACW's Mother's Club in that city, and an active member of the Urban League. Dr. Mary Etter Potter, a 1907 graduate of the Na-

tional Medical College in Louisville, specialized in gynecology and obstetrics, and served as the medical examin-
er for five women's organizations in that city. Dr. Lillian
Singleton Dove, a 1917 graduate of Meharry, was probably
the first Black female surgeon. She wrote regular columns
for the *Chicago Defender* called "Health Briefs," and
served as the chairperson for the Scientific Staff of the
Woman's Section of the World's Fair in Chicago in 1928.

Dr. Lucie Bragg Anthony, another Meharry graduate,
class of 1907, became the supervisor of county schools in
Sumter, South Carolina, doing health work, literacy work,
and teacher training in the rural areas of the county. During her tenure she was instrumental in establishing twenty-seven new schools in the area.

Dr. Alice Woodby McKane created a training school for
nurses in southeast Georgia in 1893, the first of its kind in
the state. During a brief stay at Private Hospital in Mon-
rovia, Liberia, she helped found the Department for the
Diseases of Women. Returning to the United States, she
founded the McKane Hospital for Women and Children
and Training School for Nurses in Savannah, Georgia, in
October 1896. In the twenties this became known as Charity Hospital.

Like Dr. McKane, Dr. Georgia E. Lee Patton from Tennessee (who graduated in 1893 from Meharry as a physician and surgeon) also traveled to Africa. Dr. Patton
chose to remain, devoting her life to missionary and
medical labors. Consciousness of the African continent
was reflected too in admissions policies to the Negro
medical schools. Of the 497 students at Meharry in 1924,
every state in the union and the African continent was
represented.

Among the most beloved of these early doctors was
S. Maria Steward (1848—1918). She studied at the New
York Medical College for Women and Children, graduating as valedictorian of her class in 1870. She interned at
the Long Island College Hospital, specializing in obstetrics and gynecology, and was the only female intern at
the time. Dr. Steward set up her own practice in Brooklyn,
New York, and according to her biographer it was "unre-
stricted by race and sex discrimination and consultations
brought her in frequent contact with leading New York
practitioners. At the zenith of her Brooklyn career she

maintained consulting offices in two widely separate sections of the city."[21] Dr. Steward practiced in New York for twenty-six years, and then became the resident physician at Wilberforce.

Along with her distinguished sister Sarah Garnet, an educator who became the first colored principal of a New York public school, Dr. Steward was an active suffragist and civil-rights leader. The sisters were the founding force behind the Equal Suffrage League, and both participated in the testimonial dinner honoring the antilynching work of Ida B. Wells, held in New York City in 1892.

Dr. Steward was a member of the United States delegation to the World Congress of Races held in London, England, in 1911. The congress brought together anthropologists, social scientists, physicians, and scholars from all parts of the globe to present scientific refutation of race inferiority theories. Dr. Steward presented a paper at the congress entitled "Colored American Women." Dr. W. E. B. Du Bois, also a delegate, reported on the congress in the *Crisis* some months later. He noted that "no paper was more eagerly listened to than that which told of the up struggling of the Negro woman in the United States,"[22] delivered by Dr. Steward.

Dr. Steward was acutely aware of the role of women in medicine, and associated herself in particular with Dr. Clemence Lozier of the New England School of Medicine for Women, a white woman who had pioneered in the admission of women to medical schools. In a paper presented before a convention of the NACW in 1914 called "Women in Medicine," Dr. Steward paid tribute to Dr. Lozier and expressed her indebtedness to the "noble band of heroic, energetic women [who] opened up the road of opportunity to the great army of women who are now following in the footsteps of their pioneer sisters."[23]

Although the state of medical practice at the turn of the century was limited in many ways, there is no evidence to suggest that the quality of care provided by Black doctors differed significantly from that offered by the profession as a whole. The motivation of many Black doctors, however, appears to be markedly different in that they were born of a community grounded in the common struggle of emancipation, and they returned to service that community and that struggle.

Fifteen years after the first Black woman received her medical degree, Mary Eliza Mahoney became the first woman of the race to receive a diploma in nursing. She was graduated from the New England Hospital for Women and Children in Boston in 1879. Although viewed as an acceptable profession for white females by the 1870s, discrimination against Black women in nursing remained virtually impenetrable until the mid-twentieth century. Nursing schools frequently refused admission to Black women, and the American Nurses' Association excluded Black members until 1951. According to a study done by the Hospital Library and Service Bureau of the American Conference on Hospital Service in 1925, of the 1,688 accredited schools of nursing in the United States, only 54 admitted Afro-Americans. Of these 54, almost half were schools of nursing connected with Black-run hospitals, or with municipal hospitals that serviced Black patients.[24]

Consequently, it was the Black community that provided overwhelmingly for the training of its own people. In 1891, Dr. Daniel H. Williams, superintendent of Provident Hospital in Chicago, established a nurses' school as part of the hospital's program. Three years later he established another nurses' school at Freedmen's Hospital in Washington. The majority of Black nurses came from these schools, and from those set up by the women doctors in the South at Meharry and Howard.

The first Black public health nurse was Mrs. Jessie Sleet Scales, a graduate of Provident Hospital. In 1900 she was appointed to the Tuberculosis Committee of the Charity Organization Society in New York City. Shortly thereafter another Black woman, Mrs. Elizabeth Tyler Barringer, a graduate of Freedmen's Hospital, had the distinction of serving as resident nurse for the famed Henry Street Settlement in New York City, run by Lillian D. Wald.

Scales and Barringer were exceptions, however. The majority of Black women were unable to secure institutional or public employment, except in Black-run hospitals. Forced into a mold of domestic servitude by racist and male supremacist constraints, most found employment only as private-duty nurses.[25] Public health nursing as a profession for Black women was supported, however, by some of the more progressive white women in social work and in the American Nurses' Association, although it was understood that their work was to be confined to colored people. The argument was that tuberculosis and other infectious diseases, rampant in the poverty-stricken Black communities, would spread to the rest of the population if it were not adequately controlled. Typical of the argument was this statement by two women from the Henry Phipps Institute of the University of Pennsylvania in Philadelphia, encouraging tuberculosis training for colored student nurses: "[In 1921] the tuberculosis death rate shows that the Negro is about four times as susceptible as the White. Since infection is not limited to any one group, it is easily seen that the well-being of the Negro is a very essential phase of the entire public health movement."[26] Others cited the contagion brought by Negro servants into the homes of the rich.[27]

In response to the segregation of Black women in the nursing professions, the National Association of Colored Graduate Nurses (NACGN) was organized in 1908, with twenty-six charter members. The association had three main goals: (1) to advance the standards and the best interests of trained nurses; (2) to break down discrimination in the profession; and (3) to develop leadership within the ranks of Negro nurses, in community and professional service. Some forty years after its founding (and after the American Nurses' Association integrated its membership, activities, and committees), the colored association dissolved itself.[28] NACGN, however, helped to establish the professional identity of Afro-American women who believed that as nurses they were in a particularly advantageous position from which to influence race relations. As one woman expressed it: "The respect the Negro nurse can win for her race through close professional contact is indeed surprising. Here she meets the masses of people; all ages, all races and creeds. It is up to her to leave a good impression on the minds of those with whom she comes in contact. She has for her material hundreds and hundreds of young minds; minds that can be shaped and impressed. It is through these that she must bring about better race relations."[29]

In spite of the years of discrimination and employment limitations, Black women in nursing contributed to the Afro-American community's work, particularly in the development of rural and preventive medicine and in midwifery. Conditions in the rural South for Black families at the turn of the century were appalling, and the vast majority of Black people lived in the South until the migrations at the world wars. Acute poverty, starvation, and malnutrition were common. There were no sanitation facilities. Disease, especially tuberculosis and influenza, smallpox and yellow fever, were widespread. Large families were crowded together in single-room shanties with dirt floors, tin roofs, and no running water or other amenities. In 1924 the average life span of a white man was forty-six years, and that of a white woman, fifty-two. For Black men the average life span was thirty-seven years, and the Black women's was thirty-nine.

Through the Black churches, the professional associations like the NACGN and the NMA, the National Association of Colored Women, and the eventual receipt of some minimal and reluctant assistance from the American Nurses' Association, the American Red Cross, and related relief agencies, Black nurses worked to improve these public health conditions in the South. Unlike many of their colleagues, however, the Black public health nurses and midwives worked outside of institutional settings, with little income and few supplies and medicines. They provided care within the daily grind of rural poverty.

Very intense racism also confronted Black people in dentistry, so much so that as late as 1880 there were less than a dozen practitioners in the entire country.[30] Until Meharry and Howard established dental schools there was no appreciable number of Negro dentists. Nevertheless, there were several Black women among the pioneers in this newly emerging and almost exclusively white profession.

The first was Dr. Ida Gray, born in Clarksville, Tennessee, in 1867. Raised and educated in Cincinnati, Ida Gray succeeded in gaining admission to the Department of Dental Surgery at the University of Michigan. She graduated in 1890, returned to Cincinnati, and established a long and successful practice.

Dr. Gertrude Elizabeth Curtis McPherson was graduated from the New York College of Dental and Oral Surgery in 1904, and became the first colored woman to pass the New York State Board of Dentistry. Vada Somerville was graduated from the Department of Dental Surgery, University of Southern California, circa 1904. (Dr. Somerville was also the first female graduate in pharmacy from that university.) Olive M. Officer was graduated from the Northwestern University School of Dentistry, circa 1905, and was ranked second in a class of 300 male students. Dr. Officer was also an active member of the Illinois chapter of the NACW, serving as the state treasurer for a number of years. However, domestic responsibilities and child rearing prevented her from practicing her profession during most of her life.[31]

In 1894 the first Black women received their degrees in pharmacy. All were Meharry graduates. They were Matilda Lloyd from Nashville, Tennessee, Margaret A. Miller from South Carolina, and Bella B. Coleman from Natchez, Mississippi. One Black woman opened her own pharmacy in New York City in 1921.[32] The two women to first practice podiatry in New York City were Black. Alma Mary Haskins, born in 1894 in Newport News, Virginia, attended New York University from 1915 to 1917, and graduated from the First Institute of Podiatry in New York City. Emily C. Charlton also graduated from the First Institute of Podiatry, in 1920, and established a successful practice in Brooklyn, New York. Her husband, Dr. Melville Charlton, was a well-known musician and had the unusual distinction of serving as organist for the religious school of the white-run Union Theological Seminary in New York.

3   In addition to the medical profession and its allied fields, Black women were also among the first women of any race to practice law. The first woman to argue a case before the United States Supreme Court was Black. Her name was Lucy Terry Prince (1730 – 1821). The case involved an effort by one Colonel Eli Bronson to steal some land from the Prince family in Sunderland, Vermont. The Princes, an unusually well-to-do Black family, retained Isaac Tichenor, later Governor of Vermont, as their attorney. Tichenor drew the pleadings but when the case reached the Supreme Court, Lucy Prince opted to argue it herself. The Hon. Samuel Chase of Maryland was Chief Justice. The case was heard in 1796, and the Princes won.

Justice Chase remarked that Lucy Terry had made a better argument than he had heard from any lawyer at the Vermont bar.[33]

In general, the legal profession was extremely difficult to penetrate, and most sources indicate that as late as 1910 there were only two practicing Black women lawyers in the United States. Charlotte E. Ray (1850 – 1911), daughter of the New York abolitionist leader Charles B. Ray, was graduated from Howard University Law School in February 1872, and thus became the first woman of the race to be awarded a law degree. She was admitted to the District of Columbia bar the following month. According to her biographer: "The District's legal code had recently been revised and the word "male" in connection with admission to the bar stricken out; her application apparently caused no debate. She seems to have been . . . the first woman admitted to the bar in the District of Columbia."[34]

Ray opened a law office in Washington, but another attorney, Kaye Kane Rossi, reported in 1897 that "Miss Ray . . . although a lawyer of decided ability, on account of prejudice was not able to obtain sufficient legal business and had to give up . . . active practice."[35]

Mary Ann Shadd Cary (1823 – 1893) was also graduated from Howard Law School, in 1884 at the age of sixty-one, after a long and illustrious career in the abolitionist movement. She devoted herself full time to her new profession and "met with notable success to the end of her life."[36]

Miss Ida B. Platt was graduated from the Chicago Law School in 1892 with high honors, but was denied admission to the Illinois bar. Fluent in German and French, Miss Platt worked during the day as a law clerk and stenographer in a prominent Chicago law firm, and pursued her own practice at night. According to historian Gerda Lerner, another Black woman named Lutie Lytle was admitted to the bar of Tennessee in 1897, with full accreditation.[37]

Several Black women distinguished themselves in the legal profession in the twenties, and were no doubt among the first women of any race to achieve the status they did. Mrs. Sadie Tanner Mossell Alexander was graduated from the University of Pennsylvania Law School in 1927, and served as associate editor of the *Pennsylvania*

Law Review in her senior year, a distinction reserved for those in the top ten percent of a graduating class. She was admitted to the Pennsylvania bar in 1928, and immediately thereafter was appointed assistant city solicitor in Philadelphia. Mrs. Alexander was also one of the first three women of the race to receive a Ph.D. She graduated from the University of Pennsylvania in 1921 with a doctorate in economics.[38]

Mrs. Clara Burrill Bruce graduated from Boston University Law School in 1926, and had the distinction of serving as editor-in-chief of the *Boston University Law Review* in her senior year.

Violette N. Anderson graduated from the Chicago Law School in 1920, and was the first colored woman admitted to the practice of law in Illinois. She was the first woman of any race to serve as assistant city prosecutor in Chicago (1922 – 1923), and was also vice-president of the Cook County Bar Association. Anderson was the first colored woman admitted to practice before the United States Supreme Court.

4   That Black women were the first women of any race to practice medicine in the South, and among the first women to enter the professional world, is explicable in terms of the historical experience of the Afro-American community. Honed in the agony of the slave experience, and yet achieving a degree of economic and psychological independence from Black men that was unknown to the majority of white women, Black women sustained a strength and resilience that allowed them to conquer an otherwise forbidden terrain.

The Black women who entered the professions at the turn of the century were acutely conscious of themselves as representatives of a race barely a generation removed from slavery. Their writings and comments also reflect awareness of themselves as women challenging the limits of sexual oppression. Supported by their communities, inspired by an optimism born of the knowledge that no matter how rough it was, nothing could be worse than slavery, they persevered. Anna Julia Cooper captured the essence of this spirit when she wrote:

Quest
for Dignity

To be a woman in [this] age carries with it a privilege and an opportunity never implied before. . . . To be a woman of the Negro
race in America . . . is to have a heritage . . . unique in the ages. . . .
The race is young and full of the elasticity and hopefulness of
youth. All its achievements are before it. It does not look on the
masterly triumphs of the nineteenth century civilization with
that *blase* world-weary look which characterizes the old washed
out and worn out races which have already, so to speak, seen
their best days. . . .

Everything to this race is new and strange and inspiring. There
is a quickening of its pulse and a glowing of its self-conscious-
ness. Aha, I can rival that! I can aspire to that! I can honor my
name and vindicate my race! This . . . is the enthusiasm which
stirs the genius of young Africa in America.[29]

Postscript   On August 12, 1977, the first Black woman in
the history of Massachusetts was sworn in as a judge.
Choosing the site for her swearing-in ceremony—the
Harriet Tubman Community Center in the heart of the
Roxbury ghetto—Margaret Ann Burnham became an associate justice of the Boston Municipal Court. Her appointment by Governor Michael Dukakis was approved
only after a grueling battle with the Massachusetts Bar
Association.

A 1969 graduate of the University of Pennsylvania Law
School, Ms. Burnham's first client was Angela Davis. She
has since defended a prisoner charged with assault in the
1971 Attica uprising, and she represented the Communist
Party of the United States in its efforts to achieve ballot
status in Massachusetts in the 1976 presidential elections.

Upon her appointment, Ms. Burnham said: "I don't
have any illusions that I can make *tremendous* changes in
the character of justice by taking this particular seat. But I
see it as *one* way to extend the struggle for human rights."

Margaret Burnham's appointment to the Massachusetts bench is a historic event. It is also, perhaps even
more, an act of poetic justice. History has its aesthetic dimension, after all.

6

Domestic Labor:
Patterns in Black and White

Some years ago, Mary Inman—whose work I had heard of, but whom I had never met—sent me a copy of an essay she had written entitled Woman-Power. *This work was published in 1942 under the auspices of a Los Angeles—based Committee to Organize the Advancement of Women. The point of the essay was to construct grounds for an argument within the framework of Marxian economics, that women's unpaid domestic labor in the home, produced—albeit indirectly—surplus value. Inman's work is not widely known, but it presaged the debate among Marxist-feminists in modern times.*

Briefly, this is the point of the debate. Attention paid in Marxist theory and practice to industrial workers ("the proletariat") is predicated upon the Marxist view of capitalism. The kernel of Marx's discovery about the nature of capitalist relations of production was in his assertion that the source of profit for the owners of modern industry was in the surplus value extracted from the workers at the point of production. The source of profit was not in the fluctuations of price, or in the alternating supply and demand of the market, but in the exploitation of the labor-power of the workers themselves. Labor-power was a commodity like any other, and workers sold their power to labor to an employer in exchange for wages.

The surplus value was appropriated in the difference between the wages paid the workers (based upon what was necessary to maintain the workers and their families) and the actual exchange value of the commodities the workers produced (based upon the socially necessary labor-time to produce them). "Exchange value" in this Marxist sense is a theoretical figure around which prices fluctuated, usually upwards, in order to inflate profits. An "exchange value" might be assigned only in the production (or transport) of commodities because only commodities were exchanged in the capitalist market.

It was from this point of view that the idea arose that only workers who contributed to the production of commodi-

ties (at whatever stage of their completion) were "productive" workers in the capitalist economy because only they produced surplus value. Others who are employed in service, clerical, or sales work are part of the working class as salaried employees and may be oppressed in various ways, but they are not part of the proletariat (unless one is a clerical worker in a factory, for example), because no "thing," i.e., no commodity, results from their labor. Within a strict interpretation of Marxian economics, the word "exploitation" means the extraction of surplus value. Thus, in this sense, only the proletariat is exploited; and only the proletariat, therefore, has the power to overturn the capitalist class. There have been, of course, many arguments and revisions over this and other interpretations of the Marxist texts. For my purposes here, I have simply tried to lay out the basic outline of the idea of surplus value.

From a feminist perspective there are many limitations in this theoretical rendering. It is not that what is said is wrong. On the contrary, an understanding of the theory of surplus value seems essential, and it is frequently helpful in analyzing the particularly exploitative position of women within the work force. The problem, however, is that it is a male-centered theory, and therefore incomplete.

First, the majority of industrial workers have been and are men. Women are concentrated precisely in service, clerical, and sales work so that our political subordination is built into even the theoretical concept of the working class. Second, domestic labor—which occupies a substantial portion of most women's time and energy—is designated as "unproductive" and apparently "nonexploitative." It remains, at least theoretically (if not practically), invisible, within the political economy of capitalism. Third, in Marxist theory, the masses of women almost always derive their class status from the men to whom they are attached. In these ways, women can claim no independent or autonomous role in the revolutionary process. Women are continually placed on the periphery of the "real" drama of history.

Women within the Marxist movement, like Mary Inman and many, many more in the modern period, who are committed to socialism, have tried to revise the theoretical structure so that woman's labor could be assigned a revolutionary potential and meaning on its own terms. This has *been the reason for the debate over domestic labor, and why the argument has turned on proving whether that labor is productive (i.e., producing surplus value) or nonproductive.*

Frustrated by the limits of the textual invocations and realizing from my own experience and that of virtually every woman I had ever known that domesticity was a charged and painful issue, and that we certainly felt exploited physically and often sexually, I wanted to approach the issue from a different point of view. In the course of thinking about this, I was struck by what in retrospect seems like an obvious point, namely, that the great majority of paid domestic workers in private service in the United States in this century have been Black women. Exploration of this reality seemed to provide another dynamic that might help to resolve the Marxist debate.

I pursued an investigation into the history of domestic service. The resulting essay did resolve the Marxist debate, at least in my own mind, by changing the categories of analysis altogether. More important, however, the work compelled a different and unexpected intent. My thrust shifted from only seeking a resolution in Marxian theory to gaining an understanding of woman's domestic servitude as a political issue in its own right. I learned in this process that our "felt" exploitation as women, Black and white, was real enough; and this confirmed a growing sense I had that women's feelings and experiences ought to stand on their own merit.

P RIVATE household work was the single most important avenue for the gainful employment of women in the United States throughout the late nineteenth and early twentieth centuries. Between 1890 and 1920, the proportion of white women engaged as domestic workers declined by one-third, while the proportion of Black women so engaged increased by forty-three percent. By the twenties, fully half of all Black women who were employed worked as domestic servants. By 1930, with the Depression, the figure rose to sixty percent.[1]

Although the overall number of domestic workers declined in the United States after 1890, it remained the most important source of work for Black women until approximately the end of the Second World War. Additionally, many Black women employed in the tobacco, crab, and textile factories in the South were only seasonal workers. They supplemented their meager earnings by doing domestic work in the off-season.

The employment of Black women as domestic servants was not a historical accident. Black women were systematically excluded from all other areas of employment except laundries, agriculture, and janitorial positions in manufacturing. Domestic employment was a confirmation and continuation of their servile status as former slaves. In this respect, the intersection of racism and male supremacy as experienced by Black women serves to clarify the special character of domestic labor within the capitalist political economy. In particular, the Black experience allows us to see the precapitalist form of the unpaid domestic labor as it is performed by all women in the society, and the impact of this domestic servitude on all women in the work force, even those employed in nondomestic spheres as clerical, service, production, and professional workers.

The employment of domestic workers in the United States was a feature of the organization of upper- and eventually middle-class family life in the late nineteenth and early twentieth centuries. This employment of domestic workers, however, was not intended to free the wealthy or middle-class woman as woman. The extent to which these women might be relieved of their domestic chores was a demonstration of the financial prowess and class status of their husbands. They were to be spared the housewives' ordeal as an ostentatious and sometimes frivolous display of male wealth, but their class status and privilege was only a reflection of their husbands'. That is, the status of these women (and all others) originated in precapitalist economic arrangements in which women along with other productive and reproductive resources, such as cultivated land and domesticated animals, were made the property of individual men.[2]

The extent to which the display of male property values rather than the emancipation of women from household drudgery was the motive force behind the employment of domestic labor is most strikingly revealed by the patri-

archal excesses of the Southern aristocracy, and its cov-
eted reputation for so-called Southern hospitality. It is
also confirmed by the testimony of Black women reporting on the absurd and unnecessary tasks they were frequently called upon to perform:

Mrs. Eisenstein had a six-room apartment lighted by fifteen windows. Each and every week, believe it or not, I had to wash every
one of those windows. If that old hag found as much as the teeni-
est speck on any of 'em, she'd make me do it over. I guess I would
do anything rather than wash windows. . . . There wasn't a week,
either, that I didn't have to wash up every floor in the place and
wax it on my hands and knees. And two and three times a week
I'd have to beat the mattresses and take all the furniture covers off
and shake 'em out. . . .[3]

That upper- and middle-class women themselves
bought into the property relationship imposed upon
them in no way negates the actuality of their own subjugation. Moreover, these arrangements were reinforced by
the propaganda that filled the pages of women's magazines and popular journals everywhere. The so-called
Domestic Science Movement of the twenties and thirties
elevated proper maintenance and care of the home to
preposterous levels of class indulgence. Consider this
sentiment in the *Ladies' Home Journal:*

Home is a place of abode of persons bound together by ties of affection; a place where affection of parents for each other, for their
children, and among all members of the family is nurtured and
enjoyed; where genuine personal hospitality is extended; where
the immature are protected and guarded. A place where one may
have rest, privacy and a sense of security; where one may enjoy
his individual kind of recreation and share it with others. A place
where one may keep his treasures; where one may satisfy his individual tastes; where fundamental culture, consisting of
customs, languge, courtesies and traditions, is conserved and
passed onto the young. A place where regard for others, loyalty,
and other worthy character traits are cultivated and enjoyed, a
haven, a sanctuary and a source of inspiration.[4]

The perfection of the home was seen as an extension of
a woman's personality, a representation of her worth as a
human being. She also assumed responsibility for presenting an appropriate display of her husband's class
status. It is no wonder that complaints and laments about
the poor quality of domestic help filled the pages of

Domestic
Labor

women's magazines for decades. The so-called servant problem was rooted in these patriarchal relations and in the fetishisms of the upper-class, not in the alleged ineptitude or laziness of domestic servants.

Although the mass employment of domestic labor in the late nineteenth and early twentieth centuries was concentrated in the South with its planter-class tradition, it became increasingly fashionable in the Northeast as well. By way of contrast, the employment of domestic servants was largely unknown in the nonurban areas of the Midwest and West where agricultural production on family farms predominated, thus placing women in a different and usually productive position within an extended family unit. Among wealthy Anglo ranchers in the Southwest, however, large numbers of Mexican women were employed as servants.

The ornamental role of upper- and middle-class white women reduced them, in fact, to a nonhuman existence. Regarded as mere objects of male pleasure and a demonstration of male wealth, they frequently treated their servants with cruel and capricious contempt in a pathetic effort to reclaim some semblance of their own dignity and worth. In this way, their upper-class bias and racist bigotry were combined with their actual degradation, to pit woman against woman in a vicious cycle of subjugation that left Black women battered and impoverished.

Writing in 1940, a Black woman described her life as a domestic worker in a Northern city in a way that particularly reveals this dynamic.

They just can't be as bad as they seem to me—these women I have worked for as a domestic. After all, I knew many fine women in various capacities before I was forced, as a penniless widow of forty, to go out to service in order to earn a living for my child and myself.

No, she can't be as bad as she seems, this average woman who hires a maid—so overbearing, so much a slavedriver, so unwilling to grant us even a small measure of human dignity. But I have had three years of experience in at least a dozen households to bear eloquent witness to the contrary.

Take this matter of inconsiderateness, of downright selfishness. No other women workers have the slave hours we domestics have. We usually work twelve and fourteen hours a day, seven days a week, except for our pitiful little "Thursday afternoon off." The workday itself is nerve-racking. Try broiling a steak to a nice turn in the kitchen while a squalling baby in the next room, in need of dry diapers, tries to protect himself from his brother, aged two, who insists on experimenting on the baby's nose with a hammer. See how your legs ache after being on them from 7:00 A.M. until 9:00 P.M., when you are finishing the last mountain of dishes in the pantry! Know how little you care for that swell dinner you cooked when it comes to you, cold, from the table at 8:00 P.M.

Our wages are pitifully small. I doubt if wages for domestics average higher anywhere than in New York City; and here $45 a month is good for a "refined woman, good cook and fond of children."

It is not only the long hours, the small pay, and the lack of privacy—we often have to share a room with the children—that we maids find hardest to bear. It is being treated most of the time as though we are completely lacking in human dignity and self-respect. During my first years at this work I was continually hopeful. But now I know that when I enter the service elevator I should park my self-respect along with the garbage that clutters it.[5]

The class character of domestic labor may be seen in considering the observation of the well-known socialist economist, I. M. Rubinow, writing on "The Depth and Breadth of the Servant Problem" in 1910 that: "the patent office in Washington is even now filled with devices that would reduce all housework to a matter of pushing buttons. Why are these not in use? Because it does not pay to market them. Why not? Because . . . there has been a plentiful supply of cheap human labor."[6]

It was not until capitalism required significantly more women in its industrial, service, and clerical work force, most notably with each of the world wars, that labor-saving household appliances were introduced and marketed on a mass scale. The modes of reproduction were dramatically altered by these technological advances, but the social relations within the household remained virtually unchanged. The impact of technology on housework is instructive because it reveals the archaic and precapitalist design of the domestic arrangement. Indeed, household labor, whether paid or unpaid and as it is performed by the mass of women in society, is precisely a private service for the capitalist class as a whole.

The electrification of homes in the United States was

completed by 1928. As early as 1920, coal and wood stoves had been largely replaced by gas, oil, and electric models. The 1920s were described by one writer as "the years of the bathroom mania," as indoor plumbing created a craze among the upper classes for recessed tubs, tiled floors and walls, brass fixtures, single-unit toilets, and enameled sinks. By 1935, in fact, most urban homes had indoor plumbing, hot and cold running water, and centralized heating. As a consequence of these and similar technologies, Frank Lloyd Wright designed the first kitchen that was not entirely a separate room, in 1934. Electrification brought with it the mass production of household appliances including electric irons, vacuum cleaners, washing machines, and refrigerators.

"The change from the laundry tub to the washing machine," wrote one scholar examining household technology, "is no less profound than the change from the hand loom to the power loom. . . ."[7] Still, there is a considerable difference between the impact of technology on domestic economy and its impact on industry.

Technology in the home decreased specialization among household workers and eliminated almost all divisions of labor. Indeed, "the housewife is just about the only unspecialized worker left in America—a veritable jane-of-all-trades at a time when the jacks-of-all-trades have disappeared. . . . She is a chauffeur, charwoman and short-order cook, . . ." among many other things.[8]

Technology did not reduce the amount of time devoted to housework,[9] and the introduction of new appliances was accompanied by an ideological campaign to keep women in the home, tied to the domestic sphere. Servants were largely eliminated in the middle class. The wife herself now assumed direct responsibility for the household labor. The decline in domestic servants, however, was not due to a decline in the demand for them. It was due to the fact that as rapidly as women could get themselves out of domestic servitude by going to work in industry, they did. The pay was better and the hours were subject to greater public regulation and scrutiny.

There was also a significant increase in the importance of consumption as an extended form of women's work.[10] A mass credit system was introduced to allow middle-class and working-class families to gain access to the new household technology. Advertising became a multibillion dollar industry with the twofold, interrelated function of selling products and reinforcing the ideology of the domesticated woman.

In short, the introduction of the new modes of reproduction was coincident with and an essential aspect of the transition from capitalism to monopoly and state monopoly capitalism. However, these new modes were superimposed on a precapitalist economic formation. Therefore, within the household they had a primarily regressive rather than a progressive impact on the household workers they affected. However, the new labor-saving technology also laid the material basis for the large-scale entrance of working-class women into the non-domestic, paid work force.

The social and economic impact of domestic servitude on all women in the work force may be seen by considering the precapitalist nature of the arrangement. Black women were the majority of domestic workers precisely as a result of their status as former slaves. For the essence of all precapitalist relations is that those who toil do not sell their labor-power to an employer for a wage; rather, they are forced to sell their labor alone. This is not simply a semantic quibble. It is the difference between those who sell only their power to labor, and those who are forced to sell their person as a condition of their labor.

In the original text of his lectures on "Wage-Labour and Capital," which Marx delivered to the German Working-men's Club of Brussels in 1847 and published as a pamphlet two years later, he used the term "labour" to describe the relationship the workers assumed with their employers. When the first volume of *Capital* was published twenty years later, Marx used the term "labour-power" to describe the same relationship. And in 1891, after Marx's death, when Engels arranged for the republication of the 1849 pamphlet, he changed the original text: "'This pamphlet,'" Engels wrote in his introduction, "is not as Marx wrote it in 1849, but approximately as Marx would have written it in 1891. . . . my alterations centre on one point. According to the original reading, the worker sells his *labour* for wage, which he receives from the capitalist; according to the present text, he sells his *labour-power*."[11]

Domestic Labor

The change reflected recognition that a new term was

needed to distinguish between capitalist and precapitalist arrangements, to distinguish between "free labor" and "slave labor." Labor-power is a commodity sold by the worker in exchange for a "living wage." The worker, Marx insisted, "must constantly look upon his labour-power as his own property, as his own commodity, and this he can do by placing it at the disposal of the buyer temporarily: for a definite period of time. By this means alone, can he avoid renouncing his rights of ownership over it."[12]

By way of contrast, it may be seen that domestic labor is labor of a particular kind. It is a private labor, a personal service, performed in the home, the logic of which inexorably presses a woman to sell her labor, i.e., her person, rather than her labor-power.

The household worker, whether paid as a domestic servant or unpaid as a wife, enters into a precapitalist, slavelike arrangement that is superimposed on an otherwise capitalist economic framework. The arrangement is not a matter of choice, and it occurs independent of the will of the individuals who may be involved in a particular relationship. That is, even in the absence of a husband from a household due to death, divorce, or the choosing of an alternative life style, domestic labor remains a private service for the capitalist class. For its private character is determined by the social relations of production and reproduction under capitalism, and not by the individual consciousness of an emancipated woman or man.

A Black woman analyzing "The Plight of Domestic Labor" in 1936 precisely described the sale of labor, as distinguished from the sale of labor-power, which is inherent in this form of employment:

Household employment is a relation between individual employer and employee. Accordingly, it is unstandardized. The household employee finds no definite wage scale based on experience, skill or amount of work required. There is no standard for the length of the working day nor the amount of work to be accomplished during that day. Overtime is rarely computed or paid. Many workers are expected to perform any service that may be required from the time of getting up in the morning until going to bed at night; "in domestic service it is the person who is hired, and not distinctly the labor of the person."[13]

Beyond the pale of capitalist relations, domestic workers have been generally excluded from social legislation such as minimum wage laws, unemployment, health, and disability insurance, workmen's compensation, safety and health regulations, and collective bargaining, which governs other work conditions under capitalism. Consequently, domestic workers have been paid poverty wages and have worked the longest hours of any section of the work force.

"The Bronx Slave Market" was the description offered by two Black journalists of the scenes they encountered in New York City in 1935. Dozens of Black women would gather early every morning at Simpson or Jerome Avenue in the Bronx. Wealthy housewives would come "to buy their strength and energy for an hour, two hours, or even a day at the munificent rate of fifteen, twenty, twenty-five, or if luck be with them, thirty cents an hour." The domestic worker, "under a rigid watch," would then be

permitted to scrub floors on her bended knees, to hang precariously from window sills, cleaning window after window, or to strain and sweat over steaming tubs of heavy blankets, spreads and furniture covers.

Fortunate, indeed, is she who gets the full hourly rate promised. Often, her day's slavery is rewarded with a single dollar bill or whatever her unscrupulous employer pleases to pay. More often, the clock is set back for an hour or more. Too often she is sent away without any pay at all.[14]

Statements by domestic workers describing their conditions of work reveal the essential qualities of the slave-like bond. Comparing her experiences as a factory worker with those she had as a domestic worker, one woman explained:

I realized that though in the shop too I had been driven, at least there I had not been alone. I had been a worker among workers who looked upon me as an equal and a companion. The only inequality I had ever felt was that of age. The evening was mine and I was at home with my own people. Often I could forget the shop altogether for a time, while as a servant my home was a few hard chairs and two soiled quilts. *My every hour was sold, day and night.* I had to be constantly in the presence of people who looked down upon me as an inferior.[15]

Another servant reported that: "We are eternally bossed; they ask us where we are going, where we have been, and what we did, and who our friends are." Another said: "Our employer feels somehow that she is our guardian and has the right to supervise all incomings and outgoings, to question us about what we do in our leisure, and to be 'mistress' as well as employer. All this meddling is usually kindly meant, but nonetheless it reduces us from the status of a free employee to that of a vassal."[16]

Attendant to this slavelike relation inherent in the domestic condition, domestic workers were treated more often than not as chattel, as mere objects, as a "natural condition of production for a third individual or community."[17] Domestic workers described their consequent loneliness and alienation, as has many a housewife and for much the same reason. Wrote one domestic servant: "What I minded was the awful lonesomeness. I went for general housework because I knew all about it, and there were only three in the family. I never minded being alone in the evenings in my own room. . . . But . . . except to give orders, they had nothing to do with me. It got to feeling sort of crushing at last. I cried myself sick, and at last gave it up. . . ."[18]

Striking a similar note another woman said: "There is no place where one is more lonely than to be alone *with people*; and that is what working in a house means to so many, though not all."[19] The same theme of objectification was depicted by Alice Childress in her satiric novel, *Like One of the Family*. In the lead sketch, the domestic worker tells her employer to "please stop talkin' about me like I was a cocker spaniel or a poll parrott or a kitten. . . . You think it is a compliment when you say, 'We don't think of her as a servant.' . . . but after I have worked myself into a sweat cleaning the bathroom and the kitchen . . . making the beds . . . cooking the lunch . . . washing the dishes and ironing Carole's pinafores . . . I do not feel like no week-end house guest. I feel like a servant. . . . [And] I am *not* just like one of the family at all!"[20]

A Southern Black woman writing of her experiences in 1912 highlighted the impoverishment of the domestic worker, as well as the unstandardized and personal nature of the work. Her account ended with a description of the sexual abuse she encountered. It is this abuse above all else that reveals the sale of personage inherent in domestic servitude:

I remember very well the first and last place from which I was dismissed. I lost my place because I refused to let the madam's husband kiss me. He must have been accustomed to undue familiarity with his servants, or else he took it as a matter of course, because without any lovemaking at all, soon after I was installed as a cook, he walked up to me, threw his arms around me, and was in the act of kissing me when I demanded to know what he meant, and shoved him away. I was young then, and newly married, and didn't know then what has been a burden to my mind and heart ever since: that a colored woman's virtue in this part of the country has no protection. I at once went home, and told my husband about it. When my husband went to the man who had insulted me, the man cursed him, and slapped him, and had him arrested! The police judge fined my husband $25. . . . I believe nearly all white men take, and expect to take, undue liberties with their colored female servants—not only the fathers, but in many cases the sons also.[21]

This woman's account also reveals the extent to which her abuse was a dispute among men. But, in this case, a racist structure prevailed and her husband had no legal protection and no claim to exclusive rights to his wife's sexual availability. A racist and male supremacist structure were combined to make the woman the disputed personage of her white employer and her husband, and she herself had no legal or moral claim to her own integrity or autonomy.

The male presumption of the sexual accessibility of household workers, white or Black, is rooted in their historic ownership of women, predating capitalism by centuries. A wife was valued property precisely because of her productive and reproductive capacity—to labor and to bear children who could also labor. Male ownership of her labor and her person compelled the woman into sexual relations. This apparently personal relationship is, in fact, socially inscribed and legally binding. It is historically constituted and culturally prescribed.

When women enter the purview of capitalist relations of production to sell their labor-power, the male boss's assumption of sexual availability remains intact. Thus, the sexual harassment of women workers under capitalism is a general condition of female employment rather than a random occurrence. It has existed since the inception of the factory system. Reports on the sexual harassment of women workers in the United States in the eighteenth and nineteenth centuries attest to this historic continuity.[22] Often the sexual harassment or degradation of women workers is an integral part of the job itself. Historically and presently, this problem is acute for women of color, and especially for Black women who were subjected to the institutionalization of rape under slavery.

A 1977 report on sexual harassment presents something of the scope of the problem in modern times:

A woman who had poured her life into an advertising career that she loved was introduced to her new department head. He made sexual propositions to her, implying that going to bed with him would help her "get to the top." She tried to refuse politely but his lewd remarks and pointed staring continued over the following months. As she kept resisting, he also began to find fault with her work. She finally complained to his superior. One week later, she was fired. After almost a year of being unemployed, she still has not been judged eligible for unemployment compensation. . . .

A waitress who worked double shifts to support her firve children was constantly subjected to customers who pinched her buttocks and breasts or reached their hands up the short-skirted costume that she was required to wear. She dodged and tried to kid them out of it as best she could, but carrying heavy trays among crowded tables often rendered her helpless. When she complained to the restaurant manager, he told her this was all part of her job; that the regular customers had worked out a betting system, with a dollar-value attributed to each part of a waitress's body that they succeeded in giving a "good feel," and that this meant business for the restaurant.[23]

Job segregation limits the overwhelming majority of female workers to certain, usually lower-paying, job classifications.[24] The segregation also has its origins in domestic servitude. As certain aspects of reproduction were socialized, the assumption of female labor prevailed. Female factory and service workers are most frequently employed in light manufacturing, food processing, meat packing, textiles, the culinary trades. Female physicians are disproportionately represented in pediatrics; and female lawyers are relegated to "family law" and "estates and trusts." As one lawyer put it: "They tell us we're good at working with widows and orphans."[25]

Moreover, with the male supremacist assumption that

men will be the economic providers, working women always have been paid approximately half the wages of men. In this way billions of dollars in excess profits have been made from women's labor, and women have been concentrated in the light industries and marginal shops where the rate of profit tends to be lower than in heavy industry, transportation, and military production.[26]

Invariably, female workers in all capacities are evaluated, retained, and/or promoted on the basis of their personal traits and characteristics rather than their competence as workers. This too originates in the domestic sphere. It is a consequence of the male assumption of privilege and service, and of the highly personalized and unstandardized character of domestic household work. Again, the problem is particularly acute for women of color who least conform to white male norms of beauty, femininity, and passivity.

A male psychologist declined to recommend a potential counselor for employment because he found her "passively seductive" during an interview. A Black woman who was a biochemist with a Ph.D. and employed in one of the largest United States corporations described her life under white male supervision. No matter how well she performed, how expert her knowledge, how competent her work, she was still treated and looked upon as a female servant. Evaluation focused on her personality, temperament, appearance, and "feminine" behavior. Normal patterns of "male" assertiveness and competence were looked upon as abnormal examples of "female" aggression and display.[27]

Recognition of the special oppression of domestic servants led to widespread reform efforts, especially by women activists who ran settlement houses, like Jane Addams's Hull House in Chicago, or organized workers, as those involved in the National Women's Trade Union League at the beginning of the twentieth century. Women in the Socialist Party, the Industrialist Workers of the World, and the National Association of Colored Women also paid attention to the domestic issue. All of these efforts had as their major thrust the intent to standardize, rationalize, and depersonalize domestic work.

Domestic Labor

In the late nineteenth century, day workers began to replace live-in servants, especially in middle-class homes.

By the end of the First World War this form of private household work had been largely established. Although the shift was primarily brought about by technological changes and external social influences, it tended to alleviate some of the worst features of domestic servitude by setting limits on the number of hours that could be reasonably worked. Still, it was not unusual for domestic workers to put in ten-, twelve-, and fourteen-hour days.

Domestic workers themselves sought union organization. The Industrial Workers of the World (IWW) chartered several locals of domestic workers before World War I. In the aftermath of the war there was a flurry of organization, largely affiliated with the American Federation of Labor (AFL):

In Los Angeles, California the "Progressive Household Club" with a membership of 75 domestic workers is still active. The club was organized for the purpose of furnishing a cheerful and welcome home for a domestic worker taking a rest or not employed for a time. It is a self-supporting home which accommodates twenty-five girls. Their recreational and education features are not startling, as the secretary writes, but they enable the girls to pass some cheerful hours out of their "hum drum" lives. This club was among 15 other domestic workers' clubs organized in 1919 and 1920. In 1919 a Domestic Workers' Alliance with a membership of 200, affiliated with the Hotel Waitresses under the American Federation of Labor, was granted a charter. During that year, the secretary of the Hotel and Restaurant Employees of America reported that this organization had established a domestic workers' union in Mobile, Ala.; Fort Worth, Texas; and Lawton, Oklahoma, in 1919. The following March a charter was granted to domestic workers affiliated with the A. F. of L. . . . The New Orleans Union, a Negro organization, was composed of about 200 members. . . . There is . . . [also] one union of domestic workers in Arecibo, Puerto Rico, affiliated with the A. F. of L.[28]

Although a general demand of union organizers was "equal pay for equal work," a Black writer noted that "the question of equal pay for equal work for domestic workers does not enter the domestic service wage problem of the South because Negroes pre-empt this field in that section."[29]

Affiliation with the craft-based American Federation of Labor did not last long for domestic unions but significant organization was undertaken by Black workers in the

1930s under the aegis of the Congress of Industrial Organizations (CIO). The most ambitious effort was that headed by Dora Jones, the Black executive secretary of the Domestic Workers' Union, which was founded in 1934 and was affiliated with the Building Service Union, Local 149, in New York City. By 1940 this organization had 350 members, seventy-five percent of whom were Black women.[30]

In 1965 the National Committee on Household Employment (NCHE) was formed to coordinate the work of national organizations interested in upgrading domestic service. NCHE organizer Edith Sloan presented a basic premise of the coordinating group: "The private household employment system is . . . a relic of slavery and indentured servitude."[31] The NCHE stressed the need for the adoption of a standard labor contract for domestic workers guaranteeing minimum working conditions and explicitly specifying work tasks.

Permanent organization among domestic workers has been resisted by both the capitalist class in general and specific employers in particular. It is hard to sustain because of the privatized, individual, and isolated nature of domestic economy. Domestic work is outside the purview of capitalist relations, while union organization is a form specific to capitalism. The most success appears possible when the domestic union can control hiring itself by establishing union-run hiring halls from which all or most domestic servants must be employed. This tactic can force a standardization of work conditions and wages otherwise unobtainable.[32] In 1974, private household workers were for the first time brought under federal minimum wage laws, after nearly forty years of exclusion; this, too, represents an important advance. Nevertheless, the permanent organization of a domestic workers' union has never been achieved, and violations of federal and state regulations are widespread and easy to perpetrate. Transient organization and legal negligence reflect the basic character of the domestic economy itself.

The large-scale entrance of women into the nondomestic work force does not, in and of itself, lead to women's emancipation. While on the one hand it provides them with a greater degree of economic independence, they also remain limited by the daily demands of domestic responsibilities, and the assumptions of servitude which the arrangement sanctions. Indeed, in the final analysis, the conditions of household workers, paid or unpaid, cannot be successfully reformed. The domestic tasks performed by women, especially in working-class families, such as caring for children, the sick, and the aged, maintaining the home, preparing meals, and so on, has relieved capital of any but the most minimal fiscal responsibility to meet these and related social needs. The super-profits realized from this domestic arrangement both at the point of production (in lower wages) and at the point of reproduction (in unpaid household and related work) must be uprooted and overturned. With the massive entrance of women into the labor force in the United States at least, revolutionary struggle will not progress without attention to the domestic sphere.

This is a form of political struggle with particularly intense personal and psychological consequences. It is, therefore, frequently trivialized, depoliticized, and otherwise resisted, especially by men enjoying the privileges of a petty proprietorship over women. It is sometimes resisted by women too, who fear rejection and pain at the most intimate level of their lives. Nevertheless, in the last half of the twentieth century historical conditions will require that a revolutionary movement assume the complex assignment of integrating the mutual emancipation of worker and woman.

7 The Matriarchal Mirage: The Moynihan Connection in Historical Perspective

I first became acquainted with Daniel P. Moynihan's popularization of the idea that Black women were matriarchs, i.e., all-powerful, domineering, sexually permissive, and aggressive women, when Angela Davis wrote her essay on the role of Black women in the community of slaves. Angela was still in jail at the time, and I was working with her, and was on the national staff of her defense committee.

In this essay, Angela Davis disputed Moynihan's claim in historical and eloquent detail. Her article was first published in the Black Scholar *in December 1971, two months before we won her release on bail. Our acquaintance with Moynihan, however, was destined to be more direct and personal as the prosecution's strategy in Angela Davis's trial unfolded. In order to understand this trial strategy, a brief summary of her case is needed.*

Angela Davis was charged with first-degree murder, kidnapping, and conspiracy to commit both. The maximum penalty for these offenses at the time of her arrest was death. On August 7, 1970, a judge, two Black prisoners from San Quentin, and their seventeen-year-old would-be rescuer were killed at the Marin County Courthouse in San Rafael, California. San Quentin prison guards opened fire on the prisoners as they attempted to escape with the judge, three jurors, and a district attorney as hostages. The prosecution was unable to place Angela Davis at the courthouse on the day of these events. In fact, she was in Los Angeles at the time, unaware of the tragic drama that was soon to engulf her life.

The evidence connecting Angela Davis to these events was circumstantial, and had she not been the subject of political controversy as a Black woman who was both a philosophy instructor at the University of California in Los Angeles and a prominent member of the Communist Party, it is likely that the charges would never have been brought against her. The evidence revolved primarily around her friendship with the young Jonathan Jackson who had attempted the rescue, and his use of several weapons regis-

tered in her name. Angela's involvement in a statewide movement in California to free three other Black prisoners known as the Soledad Brothers was the decisive link, however, in the prosecution's mind. Jonathan's older brother, George Jackson, was one of the three Brothers. These prisoners had been accused of murdering a white prison guard at Soledad state prison. They were subsequently found not guilty. But George Jackson never stood trial. He was killed by prison guards at San Quentin in August 1971. The prosecution's case rested upon establishing that Angela Davis's motive in Marin County was ultimately to free George Jackson, by whatever means necessary.

Without direct evidence of Angela Davis's participation in the Marin County events, the issue of her motive was the key one in the case. The Moynihan doctrine became the cornerstone of the prosecution's trial strategy. Angela was portrayed as the epitome of the Black matriarch—criminal, scheming, without morality. Her devotion to George Jackson was turned into a mindless lust that drove her to murder and mayhem. Her friendship with Jonathan was transformed into a manipulative and conniving contrivance for her own evil purposes. In short, according to the prosecution, Angela Davis's motives were lust and the desire for power—precisely the images conjured by Moynihan's matriarch. It was a vicious brew to be endured and overcome. We saw it coming, of course, and when Angela Davis delivered her opening statement to the jury, she explicitly repudiated the ideological underpinnings of the prosecution's case.

Angela endured. She was found "not guilty" on all counts on June 2, 1972. Some weeks after the trial I became friends with the foreperson of the Davis jury. Mary M. Timothy told me that the eight (white) women on the jury never bought the prosecution's main line. However much some of them might have weighed the circumstantial evidence against Angela, Mary said, her guilt receded beyond all doubt before the matriarchal mirage. The matriarchal myth about Black women as fiendish and conniving manipulators might persist abstractly in peoples' minds, I concluded, but confronted with Angela Davis's presence, it failed.

It seemed to me that ideological themes such as the Moynihan idea of the Black matriarch come as the result of some felt need on the part of the men who write them. This assumption—namely, that ideology derives from social conditions—led me to look for changes in the social conditions of Black women in the post — World War II period that might help to explain the origin and popularity of the Moynihan myth. I knew from my experience in Angela's trial that it was an idea that caused deep pain. I knew also that it did great personal damage in relationships between white and Black women. I thought that if we could get some insight into the dynamic of the myth and the reasons for it, we would help to heal some wounds. As I wrote the essay that follows, I also found much cause to rejoice in the collective strength of Black women, and the power which that strength bestows upon all of us.

EULA M. Love lived in the Watts ghetto in Los Angeles. She was the mother of three children. Her husband had died of sickle cell anemia in July 1978. Neighbors said that she was having a hard time making ends meet. They had attempted to get help for the family from community agencies, but without success. Mrs. Love owed $22 to Pacific Gas and Electric Company for her utilities. On January 3, 1979, a PG&E representative went to the Love home and informed her that he was going to shut off her gas and electricity. It was the middle of winter. Mrs. Love drove the representative off her property with a shovel; then she went to a local store and obtained a money order for $22 to pay the bill.

An hour later, the PG&E representative returned to the Love home, accompanied by two police officers. They came to shut off the gas and electricity. Mrs. Love explained that she would pay the bill. She would not allow the men to shut off her utilities. She was not armed. In the altercation that followed Mrs. Love was shot by the police officers eight times in full view of her youngest daughter.

Despite massive protests in the Black community, the police officers were not indicted on criminal charges. The killing of Mrs. Love was ruled a "justifiable homicide." Only in the context of a society in which the Black woman has been cast as a criminal element is it possible to understand the killing of Mrs. Love.

In the mid-sixties, at the height of the civil-rights movement, a veritable barrage of academic eloquence announced the mariarchal despotism of the Black woman.
A report, *The Negro Family: The Case for National Action*,
was prepared by Harvard professor Daniel P. Moynihan
under the auspices of a presidential commission. The report explained that the Black woman was the dominant
figure in the Negro family, a matriarchal arrangement that
could be traced back to slavery. The slave system had
robbed the Black family of a stable and affectionate male
presence, and the Black woman had emerged as the controlling figure. Female dominance, Moynihan concluded,
had created a "tangle of pathology." This disintegration of
Negro family life was responsible for the chaos, promiscuity, drug abuse, and crime that allegedly afflicted the Negro family.[1]

The Moynihan remedy called for the introduction of
patriarchal relations in the Black community, identical to
those obtaining in the dominant culture. The Black
woman was to be dragged, for the first time, into her own
kitchen. In the meantime, the report recommended, the
government should assume a posture of "benign neglect"
until the Black community put its own house in order.
Federal funds for poverty relief programs, recreation, and
special education were useless, Moynihan maintained,
until a dominant male presence in the family was
assured.

In alleging that female dominance was the source of
poverty and crime in the Black community, the Moynihan
report necessarily cast the Black man as an obsequious
and impotent antihero. Unable to fulfill his "manly" obli-
gations, he might flail at the system like a Don Quixote, but
would find himself stripped of his "masculine" armor.
As one liberal writing in the Moynihan vein confidently
reported:

Slavery emasculated the Negro males, and made them shiftless
and irresponsible and promiscuous by preventing them from asserting responsibility, negating their role as husband and father,
and making them totally dependent on the will of another. [After
Emancipation] there were no stable families, no knowledge of
even what stability might mean, huge numbers of Negro men
took to the roads as soon as freedom was proclaimed. . . . Thus
there developed a pattern of drifting from place to place and

woman to woman that has persisted (in lesser degrees, of course) to the present day.[2]

The Moynihan report criminalized the Black woman, turning her strength into betrayal. It was she who enforced the structure of poverty and delinquency by robbing Black men of employment and Black children of a stable home life. In this way, the Moynihan doctrine evoked the ancient theme of betrayal that has always been rendered a peculiarly feminine trait. The racist/male supremacist rendition cast the victim as culprit. She was the potential or actual traitor of her people.

Traitors are criminals, and unrepentant criminals are punished. Black women are arrested, tried, and convicted for alleged criminal offenses in numbers far out of proportion to their numbers in the population. Black women are sentenced to longer prison terms than their white counterparts. Black women are sentenced to death; white women rarely draw such a severe penalty.[3] Assaults on the reproductive rights of all women acutely affect women of color, extending from cuts in medicaid for federally funded abortions to the forced sterilization of welfare mothers and children.[4]

In criminalizing the Black woman, racist ideology also intensified the male supremacist practices inflicted on all women. The escalation of violence against women in the form of rape, battery, pornography, and exorcisms performed to cast out devils augurs critical danger. Implicit in the Moynihan doctrine is also an indictment against all women. It is a warning to white women that if they persist in entering the work force as their Black sisters have done, and join with them in demanding equal pay for comparable work and related benefits in order to secure financial independence for all women, they too will endanger the basic structural unit of society—the nuclear family under male provision. In this way, white women invite social chaos and economic ruin, and they too will pay the penalty for such a transgression. These are some of the ways in which historically generated racist and patriarchal patterns are now reasserting themselves in new and forbidding detail.

The Moynihan doctrine was neither a historical accident nor the innocent blunder of a stupid man. It represented a necessary adjustment in racist/male supremacist ideology to correspond to the actual shift in the position of Black women in society.

Relegated to the fringes of the economy as agricultural sharecroppers and domestic servants until the Second World War, Black women were beyond the purview of capitalist relations of production. In the post—World War II era, however, there occurred a qualitative shift in the employment patterns of Black women. They penetrated industrial, service, and clerical jobs in large numbers. For the first time Black women were allowed to enter the mainstream of the capitalist work force. The result was a noticeable increase in the economic and political power of Black women.

It is in the context of this historic shift that the full implications of the matriarchal theory can be understood. Women have traditionally played a significant role in the history of Afro-American people. From the antislavery and woman's rights movements of the nineteenth century to the Reconstruction and post-Reconstruction battles against lynching and for land, education, and suffrage, the presence of Black women has been an appreciable force.

The difference marking the experience of Black women in the years after the last world war has not been in their subjective desire to fight, but in their objective capacity to deliver significant blows. This capacity stems from the combined impact of the consolidation of industrial unionism, the urbanization of Black people, and the proletarianization of Black women.

The Moynihan report, timed to have an impact on the civil-rights movement at its apex, sought to turn the Black community in on itself by introducing a sexual battle that had hitherto not characterized the Black experience. Moynihan assaulted the woman because she was at once the most vulnerable, given the general oppression of women in society, and, at the same time, potentially the most dangerous, for it was she who represented a new source of power in the freedom movement.

Marking the Black woman as matriarch is exactly opposite to an accurate portrayal of her experience. A matrilineal line of descent was legally imposed on the slave community in the United States by the slaveholding class. This was done in order to insure the slave status of offspring born of a slave mother and a white father (frequently the master). Here matriliny was not a function of matriarchal dominance; it was a function of institutional rape.[5]

Under slavery the Black woman was made the property of her master in the double sense of being both woman and slave. His sexual prerogative thus had a dual nature because she was a sexual object for his personal proclivities and his economic necessities. "Slave breeding," as Frederick Douglass remarked in 1850, "is relied upon by Virginia as one of her chief sources of wealth."[6] In the experience of the slave woman in the United States, matriliny signified her utter and bitter subjugation.

There were times when Black women committed suicide and infanticide rather than see themselves or their children remanded to slavery. Surely the fugitive woman Margaret Garner, who crouched in the corner of a log cabin in the winter of 1856 and slit her infant daughter's throat, and then tried unsuccessfully to kill herself and her other three children, cannot be viewed as a reigning despot.

Under slavery Black women tried as best as they could to provide for their families. Provision required strength. It is highly instructive to appreciate the extent to which white men have mistaken strength for dominance. Sociologist Joyce Ladner placed the issue squarely: "The problem is that there has been confusion of the terms *dominant* and *strong*. All dominant people must necessarily be strong, but all strong people are not necessarily dominant. Much of this misconception comes from the fact that women in American society are held to be the passive sex, but the majority of Black women have, perhaps, never fit this model, and have been liberated from many of the constraints the society had traditionally imposed on women."[7]

Historian Herbert Gutman proposed three measures of matriarchy as a form of household and family organization: (1) the degree of male presence in the family; (2) the presence of older female relatives in the household; and (3) the earning power of women as contrasted with men. Conclusions based on Gutman's research as well as on other studies show that while female-headed households will be found more frequently in Black than in white families, at least seventy percent of Black families are now, and have been consistently, double headed.[8]

In other words, it is one thing to say that the female-headed household occurs among a greater proportion of Black families than white families. It is quite another thing to allege that Black women as heads of household are *characteristic* of Black families. Moreover, studies have also shown that the percentage of Black and white families headed by women has been identical in certain historical periods. Finally, the evidence is incontrovertible that the majority of Black women have always earned less than the majority of Black men—indeed, Black women have earned the least of all workers, including white women.

The above historical information is presented in the interest of accuracy, and in order to show the racist and male supremacist biases in documents like the Moynihan report. It is not presented as an argument favoring male heads-of-household as a normative model—a discussion beyond the scope of the present essay. It should be noted, however, that latest census figures show that a growing percentage of families of all races in the United States are female-headed and that only about sixteen percent of all families in the United States include fathers as the *sole* wage worker.

The vast majority of Black people are now and have always been workers, first as slaves and then as freed men and women. And, unlike their white counterparts, the majority of Black women have always labored outside the home. Angela Davis described the unique character of the Black woman's experience in the United States, in this way: "[Although] she was a victim of the myth that only the woman with her diminished capacity for mental and physical labor should do degraded household work . . . the alleged benefits of the ideology of femininity did not accrue to her. She was not sheltered or protected, she would not remain oblivious to the desperate struggle for existence unfolding outside the 'home.' She was also in the fields alongside the man. . . ."[9]

Today, for the first time in history, a majority of women in the United States are gainfully employed outside their own homes. The phenomenal growth in female employment has been primarily due to the dramatic increase in the number of white women workers. As one economist observed: "The labor force participation for white women more than doubled between 1890 and 1960, increasing from 16.3 percent to 33.7 percent, while that for nonwhite women remained almost constant (39.7 percent to 41.7 percent)."[10] There has been, however, a very dramatic shift in the employment patterns of Black women.

Historically, Black women have constituted a marginal labor force on the fringes of the economy eking out an existence on less than survival wages. As victims of both racism and male supremacy, Black women have been able to get only those jobs considered unfit for white men, white women, and Black men. They have suffered the highest unemployment and underemployment rates among an adult population, received the lowest wages, done the most menial jobs, and enjoyed the least seniority and the least stability in employment. From the end of slavery until the 1940s the vast majority of employed Black women were forced into agricultural, domestic, or laundry work (or allied fields). Black women were totally excluded from even the most menial factory labor until the end of the First World War, with the exception of the Southern crab, tobacco, and textile factories where they continued doing the unskilled, seasonal, factory work they had done since slavery.

The 1890 United States Government Census Report showed 975,530 colored women (Black, Indian, Chinese, and Japanese) gainfully employed outside the home. Roughly forty percent of these women were agricultural workers; thirty percent were servants (cooks, chambermaids, and so forth); fifteen percent were laundry workers; and just under three percent were in manufacturing and mechanical pursuits.

Between 1910 and 1920, 48,000 Black women entered factory work. Many of these factories were recently mechanized steam laundries. Factory employment in this case did not mean a shift in occupation but only a shift in technology and organization. Black women also entered the garment industry and some light manufacturing in small numbers at the end of World War I. And in the 1930s and 1940s small numbers of Black women entered the food industry, especially in meat slaughtering, packing houses, and crab and peanut factories. This reflected their historic connection to agricultural work.

In 1920 the median wage for a Black female factory worker was $6 a week, or $312 a year. Ten years *earlier*, the average per capita income for men working full time had been $631! In other words, in 1920 a Black woman factory worker (the highest paid worker among nonprofessional Black women) was earning half of what men had earned ten years earlier.

In 1920, one-half of all Black women employed were doing domestic work, and by 1930 the number had increased to sixty percent. Nevertheless, it was not always easy for Black women to get jobs as domestic servants. For example, in Detroit in 1922, eighty to ninety percent of the calls for domestic workers were for white women, and a similar pattern had presented itself in Southern cities in the previous decade. The reason was a fad in white upper- and middle-class homes for immigrant—especially French and Swedish—help.[11]

The Second World War and the massive Black migrations from the South in the following decade dramatically altered employment patterns for Black women. By 1960 only thirty percent of employed Black women were in domestic work, although they still represented two-thirds of all domestic workers. In that same year, only twelve percent of *all* Black workers were employed in agriculture, the majority of whom were men. By 1972 only three percent of Black workers were agricultural.[12] Likewise, by 1973 only twenty percent of Black women were employed as domestic workers.

By the mid-sixties, at about the same time that the Moynihan report was released, the change in the employment patterns of Black women was discernible. In shifting from domestic and agricultural work, the overwhelming majority of Black women had become service, clerical, and industrial workers. Between 1960 and 1970, "nearly one-fourth of employed black women changed occupations, shifting the occupational distribution of black women toward clerical occupations and female dominated professions" (e.g., nurses, teachers, and librarians, according to a recent study). Current figures show that forty-three percent of employed Black women are service workers, and twenty-one percent are in clerical positions. By 1973, over seventeen percent of all industrial workers in the United States were Black women.[13]

Even more striking, in a way, is the extent to which these figures and trends hold for Black men and women returning to the South. Migration patterns have also changed. Between 1970 and 1973, 247,000 Black people moved to the South, while only 166,000 moved from the South. Of those moving to the South, nearly two-thirds had lived there before. Still, the vast majority of these people were returning to Southern cities and obtaining urban employment as service, clerical, and factory workers, and laborers.[14]

Despite the new trends in employment, the earning power of Black women remains far below that of white men and women and Black men. This has been historically true. Thus, in 1977, the median income for full-time workers was as follows: white males, $15,378; Black males, $10,602; white females, $8,870; and Black females—$8,290. It should be noted that Black men not only earn more than Black women, they also earn more than white women. Furthermore, the gap between the wages of white and Black women is lessening but there is a general tendency for both to decline relative to the earning power of white men.[15]

While the shift in employment for Black women marks a significant advance in their general position in the socioeconomic arrangement, they remain in relatively poor, intensely exploitative, and oppressive conditions compared to those of other workers. According to one astute observer:

In industry, women are more likely than men to work for marginal businesses characterized by small size, low capital investment, low profit margins, haphazard personnel practices, high employee turnover and low pay. Many thousands of women still work in such plants, making cheap clothing, costume jewelry, paper hats and party favors, inexpensive toys, picture frames, knickknacks and similar products. Sometimes ignored by government and union alike, these are the plants where conditions are most reminiscent of the last century, even to the crudely lettered "Operators Wanted" sign on the door. Usually located in old buildings in run-down neighborhoods, they draw upon the least educated and neediest portion of the labor supply: Puerto Ricans, Negroes, Mexicans and poor white migrants from the rural South....[16]

The Matriarchal Mirage

The United States Department of Labor conducted a wage survey in 1961 of twenty-seven cities which revealed that thirteen percent of the pantry-women in eating and

drinking places, and nineteen percent of the chambermaids in hotels and motels were earning less than a dollar
an hour. In one city the hourly rate for chambermaids was
forty-six cents; in another, dishwashers were also averag-
ing forty-six cents an hour.[17]

Two years later another survey, this one conducted by
the Bureau of Labor Statistics, disclosed that about half of
the 2.5 million women in nonsupervisory jobs in retail es-
tablishments in the United States earned less than $1.25
per hour, and that ten percent were earning less than a
dollar an hour.[18] As a result of these surveys the President's Commission on the Status of Women recommended extension of the Fair Labor Standards Act to
cover employment categories subject to federal jurisdiction, but not covered by it at the time.

Although these conditions have improved to some degree in the intervening years, it is clear that with employed Black women still having a median income of only
$8,290 in 1977, they constitute one of the most severely ex-
ploited sections of the working class. The significance of
the shift in Black female employment does not rest in the
amount of money earned per se, but in the nature of the
relations Black women have assumed to the means of
production.

As domestic workers Black women were isolated in private homes, and beyond the pale of any protective legislation for workers. Wages and hours were at the whim of
their employers. Plagued by exhaustion, isolation, and legal neglect, the union organization of domestic workers
was extremely difficult.

Likewise, agricultural workers locked into a sharecrop-
ping/plantation system were forced into a servitude that
resembled a semifeudal arrangement. The workers lived
on land owned by others, were dependent on the land-
lord for shelter, food, and seed, and were not paid wages
at all, but rather a cash settlement of a portion of the value
of their crop after it had been sold on the market. Debt and
continual impoverishment were not incidental or transitory features of this system but an institutional and integral part of it.

As a Southern Black woman explained it: "The economic efficiency of the plantation system is not translated into
better living conditions for the unskilled agricultural la-

borers."[19] On the contrary, economic efficiency frequently led to greater impoverishment in the drive for maximum profits by the landowners.

Cut off from the economic mainstream, the organizational potential and political power of agricultural and domestic workers was extremely limited. Saddled with a racist structure that had successfully segregated and disfranchised the Black population and with male supremacist institutions that had successfully limited women's social intercourse, the isolated, often militant struggles of Black women met with all-too-frequent defeat.

With the shift in the economic position of the mass of Black women, however, their political power as an organized force in society was gradually, but perceptibly altered. The Moynihan matriarch was an invention to counter the new conditions of increased female power, as the expanding influence of the Black woman not only enhanced her own fighting chances but also increased the political and economic weight of the Black community as a whole.

The shift in the employment patterns of Black women came largely as the result of conscious efforts by the Black community to break the shackles of servitude and poverty. With the emergence of the Congress of Industrial Organizations (CIO) in the 1930s, large numbers of Black workers, including thousands of Black women, were organized into unions for the first time. The CIO, unlike its more conservative counterpart, the American Federation of Labor, was committed to the organization of *all* workers, including the unskilled and semiskilled mass of production-line and service workers.

Writing in 1941, Sabina Martinez, Black organizer for the Amalgamated Clothing Workers of America, explained the impact of the CIO on the lives of Black women:

Negro women workers welcomed the birth of the CIO . . . and are now part of such unions as: Laundry, Cleaners and Dyers, Textiles, Teachers, Domestic and others. Negro women helped to lay the basis for these unions and in many instances were on the first committees that helped to formulate the policies of the unions. . . .

The laundry workers were unorganized for thirty years in the city of New York. In six months the CIO has organized this industry into a compact body of some 27,000 laundry workers, the great majority of whom are Negro women. Negro women helped lay the foundation, formulate the policies and now hold executive offices in the union, which is affiliated with the Amalgamated Clothing Workers of America.

The Cleaners and Dyers Union which is only five years old was given its first impetus toward the CIO by Ida J. Dudley, a Negro woman. Seeing the need for organization in the field she started to round up the clerks, being able to organize a vast number of them. The textile and domestic workers, who are partially organized, have brought into the ranks of organized labor hoards of miserable, exploited workers who are denied protection under Social Security or State Labor Laws. Dora Jones, backed by many progressive labor groups, is preparing an extensive drive for the organization of domestic workers.[20]

In addition to the CIO, the Black community created its own organizations to deal with the special forms of oppression encountered daily. The National Negro Labor Council (NNLC), for example, was founded in 1951, and emphasized equal rights for Black women. Octavia Hawkins, a member of the United Auto Workers Local 453 in Chicago, was one of its founders.

Largely under Hawkins's leadership, the NNLC undertook several campaigns to gain employment for Black women in areas hitherto closed to them, including the meat packing and electrical industries, and retail sales. Swift, Armour and Wilson, Sears, Roebuck and Company, Woolworth's and General Electric were among the companies awarded special attention by NNLC organizers. Some concessions were won, although the council was unable to crack the barriers of sexual and racial segregation in these industries in the South. Further NNLC efforts were directed toward ending discriminatory hiring practices in the tobacco and food processing industries where Black women had long been employed.[21]

In the early 1960s, significant efforts by the burgeoning civil-rights movement focused on ending the discriminatory hiring practices of selective companies. Woolworth's, Kresge's, and other chain stores were picketed from coast to coast. In San Francisco hundreds occupied the lobby of the Sheraton-Palace Hotel on successive weekends until the San Francisco hotel industry negotiated an agreement with the Ad Hoc Committee to End Discrimination.

From its inception, then, the modern civil-rights movement was committed to changing the employment opportunities for the mass of Black people. Likewise, the efforts of Black workers, notably Black women in the South, strengthened the crusade against segregation and for the franchise.

The connection between the class struggle and racial struggle is peculiar to workers of color. It means in essence that the struggles of Black workers inevitably take on the character of movements for national liberation. In the case of women, a multiple dialectic—challenging class, racial, national, and sexual oppression—presents itself. It is for this reason that the actions of Black women portend a socioeconomic impact far beyond the apparent resolution of the immediate issues of struggle. Two strikes led by Black women, one against the R. J. Reynolds Tobacco Company, and the other by Charleston hospital workers illustrate the point.

On May Day 1947, 10,000 workers, members of Local 22 of the Food, Tobacco, Agricultural and Allied Workers of America (FTA) struck the R. J. Reynolds Tobacco Company in Winston-Salem, North Carolina.[22] Eighty percent of the workers were Black. The strike was led by Moranda Smith, a Black woman who served as the local's educational director. After the 1947 strike Smith became an international representative of the FTA and its Southern regional director. She was the first woman of any race to become a regional director for an international union. She served in this capacity until her untimely death, at the age of thirty-five, in 1950.

In 1947, the R. J. Reynolds Tobacco Company was the second largest tobacco manufacturing company in the United States, and the third largest in the world. Working conditions had remained virtually unchanged in the tobacco industry since the days of slavery, with a rigid race-segregated occupational pattern.

All skilled and supervisory jobs were held by white men. Machine shredding and other machine operations were done by white men. Boxing and packing were jobs for white men and white women. Cigarette machines were operated by white women, who also did the weighing and counting. Black men did the cleaning and sweeping, made containers, and lifted and handled shipments. Black women were responsible for the hand stemming, shredding, and blending. All these operations were carried out in separate buildings.

All the seasonal workers at the Reynolds plant were Black, and the majority were women. Black women working in the tobacco industry, therefore, frequently had to supplement their earnings by doing domestic work in the off season. In addition: "There were no lunch facilities; the workers ate outside regardless of the weather. No respect whatsoever was shown for workers, particularly Black workers, by the foreman. It was not uncommon for a foreman to go into the restroom and tell Black women to return to work. Most of the foremen, former chain-gang leaders, kept guns in desks in the plant. Foremen tried to force Black women to have sexual relations with them. There were no vacations, no seniority, no paid holidays, no sick leave."[23]

At the time of the strike white women at Reynolds were earning fifty-seven cents an hour. Black women averaged forty-five cents an hour. The key demand in the strike was for a fifteen cent per hour across-the-board wage increase for all workers. The strike lasted thirty-eight days. In the end a twelve cent increase was won. But this tells only part of the story.

The strike demands were won because the workers at the R. J. Reynolds plant had the support of the CIO in other parts of the country. Strike benefits, political pressure, and moral support were essential elements in the Reynolds victory. Moreover, the workers had the organized support of the civil-rights movement, led by the NAACP. The Black community in North Carolina and throughout the South supported them.

The strike not only won a wage increase. It also resulted in the political organization of the Black community in Winston-Salem. Before the strike, 163 Black people had been registered to vote. After the strike there were 8,000 Black people registered to vote. In the next election a Black alderman was elected to the city council for the first time since Reconstruction.

Another dramatic example of the role of Black women in the forging of new ground in the civil-rights and labor movements was provided by the 1969 strike of 450 hospital workers in Charleston, South Carolina. This strike, which lasted over four months, was led by a Black woman,

Mary Moultrie, the President of Local 1199 B of the Hospital Workers' Union.[24]

Before this strike was won, half the workers had been arrested, night riders terrorized the Black community, the governor imposed a 9 P.M. curfew on the City of Charleston (to effectively ban night meetings) and he called out two battalions of the National Guard, who were augmented by hundreds of state troopers and city policemen, to enforce it.

The strike began when twelve workers were fired by the state-owned South Carolina Medical College Hospital. Those fired had been among the most active in organizing the nonprofessional licensed practical nurses, nurse's aides, kitchen helpers, laundry workers, maids, and orderlies. The twelve were dismissed on March 20, 1969, and on the same day, 450 other workers in the hospital walked out in protest, and the strike was on. The demands were: (1) union recognition; (2) an end to discrimination in wages and hiring practices; and (3) the rehiring of the twelve workers who had been fired.

A local judge promptly issued an injunction limiting the number of pickets at the hospital to "ten people picketing at a time—twenty yards apart." Although the United States Supreme Court had previously ruled such injunctions to be unconstitutional this one was enforced, and more than 150 people were arrested during the early weeks of the strike. Bail for those arrested was set at $500 for the first offense, $1,500 for the second offense, and $5,000 for the third.

The union called upon the Black community, the civil-rights movement, and its parent union in New York City for support. In response, the Southern Christian Leadership Conference (SCLC), then under the leadership of the Reverend Ralph Abernathy, sent a half dozen organizers into Charleston. The Reverend Andrew Young, then part of the SCLC staff, organized press conferences, television appearances, and mass meetings, all of which served to bring the issues of the Charleston strike to a nationwide audience. The Black community began a boycott of downtown stores in Charleston in the last week of April, which continued for the duration of the strike. On Mother's Day, some 15,000 people participated in a march through downtown Charleston in support of the hospital workers.

The Matriarchal Mirage

In the ranks were Coretta Scott King, Ralph Abernathy, and Walter Reuther, President of the United Automobile Workers of America.

The continued intransigence of the hospital and state administrations forced the union and the SCLC leadership to broaden the scope of their strike strategy. Hoping to force other segments of South Carolina industry to press for a favorable settlement of the strike, Mary Moultrie and Ralph Abernathy called for a nationwide boycott of the South Carolina textile industry and for the organization of a sympathy strike by the longshoremen that would close the port of Charleston. As the machinery for these efforts was put into gear, the hospital and state administrations were finally moved. They made a few concessions, retracted them, maneuvered, and then finally conceded defeat. It had taken 113 days to win a twenty cent hourly increase (from $1.30 to $1.50) for the lowest paid of the hospital workers, reinstatement of the twelve workers originally fired, and the establishment of mechanisms for union recognition.

As in the case of the Reynolds strike, much more than that was won. The Black women of Charleston had inspired a movement that shook the very foundations of the Old South. The Charleston strike came in the midst of the nationwide civil-rights campaign to end poverty in the United States. Conscious of the intimate connection between their own struggle and the SCLC's "Poor People's Campaign" begun the previous year, the hospital workers themselves announced their goal at the beginning of their strike: "Let us end poverty in Charleston (our own)." As one writer expressed it, analyzing the impact of what happened in Charleston:

To the working poor, especially the low wage urban workers employed in service industries, the Charleston Hospital strike is a beacon light. Its significance is heightened precisely because it occurred within the larger context of SCLC-led "hunger Marches" in Alabama, Mississippi and Illinois and demonstrations by the National Welfare Rights Organization in many parts of the country. Charleston forged a unity between the community-organizing techniques developed during the civil rights era of the Freedom Movement and the working class organizational techniques of strike action developed by the labor movement. This is an effective combination of applied techniques which will undoubtedly be sharpened by experience in the months ahead. One of the special qualities to be noted in the Battle of Charleston is that this experience tested and proved, once again, the tenacity and fighting spirit of women workers when confronted with the arrogant power of The State.[25]

Black women were also the driving force behind many of the civil-rights activities that marked the post—World War II decades. The National Council of Negro Women (NCNW), organized in December 1935 by Mary McLeod Bethune, was probably the single most important organizational force among Black women. An educator, organizer, and devoted partisan of her race, Mrs. Bethune was the founding president of what is today called Bethune-Cookman College located in Daytona Beach, Florida. During the Second World War, Mrs. Bethune was the only woman to serve in Franklin Delano Roosevelt's "Black Cabinet" and she was the director of the Minority Affairs Department of the National Youth Administration. With her energy, leadership, and prestige Mrs. Bethune forged a national unity among Black women that might have been otherwise unobtainable. Although civil-rights historians tend to see the NCNW as a social club and church-based movement rather than a political association, it was, in fact, all three, and served as an essential agency for civil-rights agitation. In the 1940s the National Council focused many of its programs and activities on the special problems faced by Black women workers—in employment, housing, child care, and federal welfare programs. In 1968 the NCNW had a national membership of 850,000.

Black women were largely responsible for the political and legal battles that broke the back of segregation in Washington, D.C. These campaigns laid the base for the civil-rights movement in the sixties. Pauli Murray, a student at Howard University Law School in the late 1930s (later to become a distinguished attorney), led a sit-in by Black students at the public cafeteria in the United States Congress building to protest segregation. Although the students were not arrested, they were refused service and physically removed from the premises. At about the same time, another Black woman, Norma E. Byrd, also located in Washington, D.C., was responsible for the founding of the Non-Partisan Lobby for Economic and Democratic Rights. Growing out of the work of a national sorority of

Black women called Alpha Kappa Alpha which had financed and conducted a free health service for tenant farmers and sharecropers in Mississippi, the Non-Partisan Lobby had as its objective the elimination of discriminatory practices and laws. It evolved into the National Non-Partisan Council on Public Affairs and became a significant antiracist pressure group in Washington through the 1940s. Likewise, in March 1946, largely through the initiative of women in the National Council of Negro Women, and a newspaper, the *Pittsburgh Courier*, a Committee for Racial Democracy in the Nation's Capital was organized to desegregate the city of Washington.[26] A few years later, the oldest and most revered Afro-American woman in the capital undertook to head the campaign that finally won the battle.

Mary Church Terrell, whose life spanned the first century of emancipation, was the founding president of the National Association of Colored Women. She was an educator, suffragist, and political organizer. At the age of eighty-six she forged a coalition of all the civil-rights and Black women's organizations in the Washington area and beyond.

Early in 1950 it came to Mrs. Terrell's attention that two antidiscrimination laws had been passed in 1872 and 1873 by the United States Congress and the Legislative Council of the District of Columbia under the administration of President Grant. The Reconstruction laws had been introduced by Lewis Douglass, who was a member of the Legislative Council and the son of the abolitionist leader Frederick Douglass. Although home rule for the District of Columbia was abolished in 1874, these two laws were never repealed.

The law of June 20, 1872, provided that: "Any restaurant keeper or proprietor, hotel keeper or proprietor refusing to sell, or wait upon a respectable, well-behaved person without respect to previous condition of servitude shall be deemed guilty of a misdemeanor, shall be fined $100.00 and shall forfeit his or her license as keeper or owner of a restaurant or hotel."

Mary Church Terrell became the founding president of an organization called the Coordinating Committee for the Enforcement of the District of Columbia Anti-Discrimination Laws. Within a year this coordinating committee had 110 affiliated organizations, 59 church affiliations, and 1,200 individual Black and white members.[27]

On February 28, 1950, Mrs. Terrell, accompanied by the Reverend Arthur Fletcher Elmes, pastor of the People's Congregational Church, Miss Essie Thompson, a member of Local 471 of the United Cafeteria Workers, and David H. Scull, a white civil-rights supporter, entered the Thompson Restaurant on Fourteenth Street, N.W. in Washington. This restaurant was selected because it was one of the largest chains serving the Washington metropolitan area.

Mrs. Terrell attempted to purchase a bowl of soup. When she reached the cashier, she was refused service and ordered to leave the premises. Mrs. Terrell brought suit against the restaurant, claiming violation of her civil rights under the 1872 law. This became known as the Thompson Restaurant Case.

For three years the case wound its way through the courts. Meanwhile, the Coordinating Committee maintained a constant vigilance with petitions, picket lines, and meetings. On July 10, 1950, a municipal court judge denied Mrs. Terrell's suit, claiming that the 1872 – 1873 laws had been "repealed by implication." She appealed. A year later, the Municipal Court of Appeals reversed the lower court and held the laws valid.

The Thompson Restaurants appealed. They were joined in this appeal by the Washington Restaurant and National Restaurant Associations. On June 8, 1953, the United States Supreme Court ruled that the antidiscrimination laws of the previous century were still valid. This case marked the judicial ending of segregation in Washington.

More than a thousand people attended the celebration of Mary Church Terrell's ninetieth birthday held, with calculated aplomb, in the Presidential Room of the Statler Hotel in downtown Washington. Mrs. Terrell died on July 22, 1954, sixty-five days after the Supreme Court decision ordering the desegregation of the public schools.

A brief capsule of civil-rights participants highlights the role of Black women in the antisegregation and voter registration drives which ended at the beginning of the seventies. Rosa Parks, the seamstress who refused to move to the back of the bus, sparked the Montgomery Bus Boycott in 1956, and a committee of one hundred Black women in

Montgomery organized a car-pooling arrangement for transportation in the Black community which provided the backbone for the boycott. Autherine Lucy was the first Black student at the University of Alabama (1955), and Dorothy Counts, at the age of fifteen, desegregated the public schools of Charlotte, North Carolina (1956).

Gloria Richardson was the chairperson of the Cambridge, Maryland, Nonviolent Action Committee. Mae Mallory led the civil-rights movement in Monroe, North Carolina. Diane Nash Bevel led the student sit-ins at Fisk University in Nashville, Tennessee, in 1960, and was the first Black woman to go to North Vietnam at the height of the war. Ella Baker, with years of experience as a field secretary for the NAACP, and an organizer for the SCLC, was the driving force behind the organization of the Student Nonviolent Coordinating Committee, and Ruby Doris Robinson served as its executive secretary. The National Council of Negro Women provided a continual, daily support network for civil-rights workers in the South through the sixties. Typical of such NCNW projects was the 1964 Wednesdays in Mississippi (WIMS), an interracial civil-rights project to establish lines of communication between Northern and Southern women.[28]

Fannie Lou Hamer was in a class by herself. She lived in Ruleville, Sunflower County, Mississippi, where Senator James O. Eastland ruled. A sharecropper for eighteen years, she was one of the first people to register to vote when the registration drive began in 1962. When she registered to vote, the plantation owner fired her and kicked her off the land.

Mrs. Hamer became a field secretary for the Student Nonviolent Coordinating Committee and then became the chief organizer of the Mississippi Freedom Democratic Party (MFDP). She led the delegation to the 1964 Democratic Party Convention that challenged the credentials of the all-white, all-male Mississippi delegation. Although the challenge failed, it was viewed by millions on national television. Fannie Lou Hamer's address at the Atlantic City Convention stunned the country. The reforms that were later introduced into the Democratic Party structure derived from the urgent need for change which she communicated. Not a few of the Black political leaders in the South today, e.g., Charles Evers, Julian Bond, and Ernest

N. Morial (the Black mayor of New Orleans), owe their political fortunes to the foundations of reform that Fannie Lou Hamer laid in 1964.

In 1965 the MFDP under Hamer's leadership organized the Mississippi Freedom Labor Union and began recruiting Black sharecroppers in the state in a drive to end their terrible poverty. A strike in May 1965 marked the first such action in the Mississippi farm lands since an abortive uprising by 'croppers in the 1930s. The strike failed, however, when the 'croppers were evicted and then forced through starvation to abandon their efforts.

Fannie Lou Hamer died in March 1977, at the age of sixty. In a tribute to her, Eleanor Holmes Norton wrote:

This profoundly black woman was of a world broader than her own race and sex. She reached out to the miserably poor whites in her native Sunflower County, organizing a cooperative farm to raise animals and vegetables. Hunger, it turned out, was the vital bond between the white and black poor. Last year, her hometown of Ruleville declared a "Fannie Lou Hamer Day." She lived to be vindicated and loved by these Mississippi whites whose hatred she had overcome.[29]

Over the death of Fannie Lou Hamer in the farm land of Mississippi, and the murder of Eula M. Love in the Watts ghetto of Los Angeles two years later, falls the terrible shadow of oppression and exploitation that has cast its mark upon the experience of Afro-American womanhood. It is the devastating alignment of white supremacist and male supremacist rule within class society. But that alignment has also produced a magnificent heritage of resistance and resilience that heralds woman's cause in profound and compelling detail.

History does not repeat itself, but our reading of history shapes our perception of the world and our vision of how to change it. With the collective rendering of woman's legacy still to come, we will reckon a course that transforms our reading of the human experience and allows us to navigate through hitherto unknown waters.

Notes

1. Woman's Legacy: A Beginning

1. Sheila Rowbotham, *Woman's Consciousness, Man's World* (Baltimore: Penguin Books, 1973), p. xi.
2. Adrienne Rich, "Disloyal to Civilization: Feminism, Racism, Gynephobia," in *On Lies, Secrets and Silence* (New York: W. W. Norton, 1979), p. 308.
3. Among many essays affirming the usefulness of materialist and Marxist analysis in feminist theory are: Christine Delphy, "For A Materialist Feminism" (paper presented to the conference celebrating the work of Simone de Beauvoir, "The Second Sex—Thirty Years Later, A Commemorative Conference on Feminist Theory," New York University, September 27–29, 1979), Nancy Hartsock, "Can There Be A Specifically Feminist Materialism" (Manuscript, Johns Hopkins University, 1980). See also Zillah R. Eisenstein, ed., *Capitalist Patriarchy and the Case for Socialist Feminism* (New York: Monthly Review Press, 1979); and Annette T. Kuhn and Ann Marie Wolpe, eds., *Feminism and Materialism: Women and Modes of Production* (London: Routledge and Kegan Paul, 1978).
4. Adrienne Rich, "Women's Studies: Renaissance or Revolution?," *Women's Studies* 3 (1976): 126.
5. Two anthologies of essays by feminist anthropologists confirm these conclusions. See Michelle Zimbalist Rosaldo and Louise Lamphere, eds., *Woman, Culture & Society* (Stanford: Stanford University Press, 1974); and Rayna R. Reiter, ed., *Toward an Anthropology of Women* (New York: Monthly Review Press, 1975).
6. This methodological approach is suggested by Joan Kelly-Gadol, "The Social Relations of the Sexes: Methodological Implications of Women's History," *Signs* 1 (Summer 1976): 809–24; and Linda Gordon, "What Should Women's Historians Do?: Politics, Social Theory and Women's History," *Marxist Perspectives* 1 (Fall 1978): 128–36. See also Gerda Lerner, *The Majority Finds Its Past: Placing Women in History* (New York: Oxford University Press, 1979, 1981).

2. Abolitionism, Woman's Rights and the Battle over the Fifteenth Amendment

1. Eleanor Flexner, *Century of Struggle: The Woman's Rights Movement in the United States* (Cambridge: Harvard University Press, 1959), p. 41.
2. Alma Lutz, *Created Equal: A Biography of Elizabeth Cady Stanton* (New York: Octagon Books, 1974), p. 144.
3. Ellen Carol DuBois, *Feminism and Suffrage: The Emergence of an Independent Women's Movement in America, 1848–1869* (Ithaca, N.Y.: Cornell University Press, 1978), p. 184. This point is the theme of the book and is especially developed in the final chapter, "The Fifteenth Amendment and Independent Suffragism." An earlier work by

Blanche Glassman Hersh suffers from a similar kind of problem. See *The Slavery of Sex: Feminist-Abolitionists in America* (Urbana: University of Illinois Press, 1978). Hersh's study contains much information and is useful because it was one of the first studies to isolate the role of women in the abolitionist movement. But among the fifty-one women included in the study, none are Black.

4. Aileen S. Kraditor, *Means and Ends in American Abolitionism: Garrison and His Critics on Strategy and Tactics, 1834—1850* (New York: Vintage Books, 1969), p. 39. A more detailed critique of these ideas is developed in my essay on woman suffrage and lynching, in this volume.

5. See the following materials in addition to citations in this chapter: Gerda Lerner, ed., *Black Women in White America: A Documentary History* (New York: Pantheon Books, 1972); Leon Litwack, *Been in the Storm So Long: The Aftermath of Slavery* (New York: Alfred A. Knopf, 1979); Sharon Harley and Rosalyn Terborg-Penn, eds., *The Afro-American Woman: Struggles and Images* (Port Washington, N.Y.: Kennikat Press, 1973); Joyce Ladner, *Tomorrow's Tomorrow: The Black Woman* (Garden City, N.Y.: Doubleday, Anchor, 1972), especially chap. 1, "Yesterday: Black Womanhood in Historical Perspective"; Dorothy Burnham, "The Life of the Afro-American Woman in Slavery," *International Journal of Women's Studies* 1 (July-August 1978): 363—77; Angela Y. Davis, "Reflections on The Black Women's Role in The Community of Slaves," *Black Scholar* 3 (December 1971): 2—16. For a useful, if brief, essay on the problem of racism in the abolitionist movement, see Herbert Aptheker, *The Unfolding Drama: Studies in U.S. History,* ed. Bettina Aptheker (New York: International Publishers, 1979), "White Chauvinism: The Struggle Inside the Ranks," pp. 120—29.

6. For the development of this theme see Herbert Aptheker, *To Be Free: Studies in American Negro History* (New York: International Publishers, 1948), esp. "Slave Guerrilla Warfare," and "Militant Abolitionism"; and Aptheker, *Unfolding Drama,* "The Civil War," pp. 81—96.

7. The most detailed study of this period will be found in W. E. B. Du Bois, *Black Reconstruction: An Essay Toward A History of The Part Which Black Folk Played in the Attempt to Reconstruct Democracy in America, 1860—1880* (1935; reprint ed., New York: Russell and Russell, 1968).

8. Frederick Douglass, *The Life and Times of Frederick Douglass* (1892; reprint ed., New York: Macmillan, Collier Books, 1962), p. 469.

9. Kraditor, *Means and Ends,* p. 48.

10. Angelina Grimké to Theodore Weld and John Greenleaf Whittier, August 20, 1837, in *The Letters of Theodore Weld, Angelina Grimké Weld and Sarah Grimké, 1822—1844,* ed. Gilbert Barnes and Dwight L. Dumond (New York: Appleton-Century-Crofts, 1934), 1:429—30; cited by Flexner, *Century of Struggle,* rev. ed. (Cambridge: Harvard University Press, 1975), p. 48.

11. Russel B. Nye, *Fettered Freedom: A Discussion of Civil Liberties and the Slavery Controversy in the United States, 1830 to 1860* (East Lansing: Michigan State College·Press, 1949), p. 251. Nye's study is an excellent resource, but he pays virtually no attention to women and their role in the civil liberties battle. A good study of the Lovejoy mur-

der is John Gill, *Tide Without Turning: Elijah P. Lovejoy and Freedom of The Press* (Boston: Starr King Press, n.d.).

12. Ira V. Brown, "Cradle of Feminism: The Philadelphia Female Anti-Slavery Society, 1833 – 1870," *Pennsylvania Magazine of History and Biography* 102 (April 1978): 145.

13. Ibid., p. 156. See also the *Proceedings of the Anti-Slavery Convention of American Women, Held in the City of New York, May 9th, 10th, 11th and 12th, 1837* (New York, 1837).

14. Sarah M. Grimké, *Letters on The Equality of The Sexes and The Condition of Women* (1838) in *The Woman Movement: Feminism in The United States and England*, ed. William L. O'Neill (Chicago: Quadrangle Books, 1969), p. 106.

15. Douglas H. Maynard, "The World's Anti-Slavery Convention of 1840," *Mississippi Valley Historical Review* 42 (December 1960): 452.

16. Cited in Herbert Aptheker, ed., *And Why Not Every Man? Documentary Story of The Fight Against Slavery in The U.S.* (New York: International Publishers, 1970), pp. 144 – 45.

17. Elizabeth Cady Stanton, *Eighty Years and More: Reminiscences, 1815 – 1897* (1898; reprint ed., New York: Schocken Books, 1971), p. 82.

18. Gerda Lerner, *The Grimké Sisters from South Carolina: Pioneers for Woman's Rights and Abolition* (New York: Schocken Books, 1971), p. 141.

19. Angelina E. Grimké, *Appeal to The Christian Women of The South* (1836), p. 3. Cited by Lerner, *Grimké Sisters*, p. 139.

20. Dwight L. Dumond, *Antislavery: The Crusade for Freedom in America* (Ann Arbor: University of Michigan Press, 1961), p. 217. Dumond also suggests that Miss Crandall closed her school "on insistence of the Reverend Calvin Philleo, whom she had recently married" (p. 212).

21. "Negroes Ask for Equal Educational Facilities, 1787," in *A Documentary History of The Negro People in The United States*, ed. Herbert Aptheker, vol. 1, *From Colonial Times Through the Civil War* (New York: Citadel Press, 1951), p. 19.

22. "Boston's Jim Crow School Is Closed, 1855," in ibid., p. 377. William C. Nell's speech was published in the *Liberator*, December 28, 1855

23. The case, *Sarah C. Roberts v. The City of Boston*, was argued before the Massachusetts Supreme Court by Charles Sumner on December 4, 1849. The complete text of his argument, which is a classic in constitutional law and was the foundation for the Brown decision by the United States Supreme Court a century later, is reprinted in full in John A. Scott, ed., *Living Documents in American History* (New York: Washington Square Press, 1964), pp. 374 – 410. The argument was published as a pamphlet in Boston in 1849. Sumner prepared another version for publication later which was printed in *Charles Sumner: His Complete Works*, Statesman Edition (Boston, 1900), pp. 51 – 100.

24. "Negro Children Speak," in Aptheker, *A Documentary History*, vol. 1, *From Colonial Times*, p. 158.

25. Louis Ruchames, "Race, Marriage and Abolition in Massachusetts," *Journal of Negro History* 40 (July 1955): 273.

26. Eleanor Flexner, *Century of Struggle*, rev. ed., p. 52. For a discussion of women's petition work in the antislavery movement see the essay by
Gerda Lerner, "The Political Activities of Antislavery Women," in her

collection, *The Majority Finds Its Past: Placing Women in American History* (New York: Oxford University Press, 1979), pp. 112 – 28.

27. Eleanor Flexner provides an excellent summary of Adams's arguments on the right of women to petition in *Century of Struggle*, pp. 51 – 52.

28. Mary Church Terrell Papers, Manuscript Division, Library of Congress, Mary Church Terrell, "Harriet Beecher Stowe," p. 9, typed manuscript.

29. Quoted in ibid.

30. The text of this speech is given in Katharine Anthony, *Susan B. Anthony: Her Personal History and Her Era* (Garden City, N.Y.: Doubleday and Co., 1954), pp. 134 – 35.

31. Harriet Carter, "Sojourner Truth," *Chautauquan* 7 (May 1889): 478.

32. Pillsbury's letter was printed by Lillie B. Chace Wyman, "Sojourner Truth," *New England Magazine*, March 1901, p. 63.

33. Ibid., p. 64.

34. Earl Conrad, *Harriet Tubman* (New York: Paul S. Eriksson, Inc., 1943), p. 36. From Conrad's account, it appears likely that Harriet herself should have been legally free. Her mother's previous owner had died very young, and had the provisions of the original will been honored, Harriet would have been born of a free woman. This no doubt influenced Harriet's thinking on her right to freedom, and the right of her sisters and brothers and parents to be free.

35. Ibid., p. 38.

36. Du Bois, *Black Reconstruction*, p. 55.

37. Conrad, *Harriet Tubman*, pp. 120 – 28.

38. See W. E. B. Du Bois, *John Brown*, ed. Herbert Aptheker (1909; reprint ed., Millwood, N.Y.: Kraus-Thomson Organization, 1973), pp. 273 – 307.

39. Conrad, *Harriet Tubman*, p. 127.

40. Du Bois, *Black Reconstruction*, p. 403.

41. Ibid., p. 8.

42. See *Proceedings of the Meeting of the Loyal Women of The Republic*, held in New York, May 14, 1863 (1863; reprint ed., New York: Emma Lazarus Federation of Jewish Women's Clubs, 1963).

43. Herbert Aptheker, "Mississippi Reconstruction and the Negro Leader, Charles Caldwell," in Aptheker, *To Be Free*, p. 171, 173. See also Suzanne D. Lebsock, "Radical Reconstruction and the Property Rights of Southern Women," *Journal of Southern History* 43 (May 1977): 195 – 216. Historian Benjamin Quarles reported that women voted in certain local elections under Reconstruction governments, in his article, "Frederick Douglass and The Woman's Rights Movement," *Journal of Negro History* 25 (January 1940): 35.

44. See, for example, Mary Frances Berry, *Military Necessity and Civil Rights Policy: Black Citizenship and the Constitution, 1861 – 1868* (Port Washington, N.Y.: Kennikat Press, 1977).

45. Stanton, *Eighty Years and More*, p. 254.

46. A rather striking example of this may be seen in the article by Laura Curtis Bullard, "The Slave-Women of America," *Revolution*, October 6, 1870.

47. *Revolution*, May 20 – 27, 1869, cited in Philip S. Foner, ed., *The Life and Writings of Frederick Douglass*, vol. 4, *Reconstruction and After* (New

York: International Publishers, 1955), p. 44. Foner's reportage of the May 1869 Convention is not completely accurate, however, and his interpretation misrepresents the division among feminists.

48. Ibid., p. 43. See also Elizabeth Cady Stanton, Susan B. Anthony and Matilda Joslyn Gage, eds., *History of Woman Suffrage*, vol. 2, *1861 – 1876* (New York: Fowler and Wells, 1882), pp. 378 – 400, for a full account of the convention proceedings. A motion very similar to Douglass's was also presented by Henry Blackwell. See *History of Woman Suffrage*, 2:384 – 85.

49. Ibid.

50. Ibid., p. 382.

51. Ibid., pp. 383 – 84.

52. The Phelps case is worth mentioning in this regard. Early in 1860 a woman named Mrs. Phelps, accompanied by a young daughter, appeared at the Albany, New York, home of a Quaker woman, Lydia Mott. Susan B. Anthony was with Mrs. Mott when Mrs. Phelps arrived. Mrs. Phelps—previously unacquainted with both women but coming to the Mott woman because she was a Quaker—explained that she had been beaten by her husband, and then divorced by him. Their children had been automatically remanded to the custody of their father. Allowed to visit the daughter, Mrs. Phelps had taken that child and fled from Massachusetts, where her husband was a state senator, and her brother a member of the United States Senate. Susan Anthony took Mrs. Phelps and her daughter to New York City late at night and in disguise. She eventually secreted them in the house of another Quaker woman, Abby Hopper Gibbons. They were successfully hidden for almost a year before detectives hired by the husband located the fugitives. In the meantime, the husband, using his political connections, had threatened Anthony with arrest unless she revealed their whereabouts. When she refused, he used his political connections in the abolitionist ranks, and both William Garrison and Wendell Phillips exerted considerable pressure to force Anthony to yield. To these men the Phelps case was a personal matter and the law was clear. To Anthony it was a political case and the law be damned. The case, and others like it often on a more personal level, presaged the deeper schism on woman's rights that was to come. See the account of this case in Anthony, *Susan B. Anthony*, pp. 156 – 58.

53. This comment was made by the adolescent son of Horace Greeley in 1871 and is quoted by Lois W. Banner, *Elizabeth Cady Stanton: A Radical for Woman's Rights* (Boston: Little, Brown and Co., 1980), p. 89.

54. With the battle for the Fifteenth Amendment successfully concluded Frederick Douglass resumed the campaign for woman suffrage, with an editorial in the *New National Era*, October 27, 1870, "Woman and The Ballot," and maintained a correspondence with Mrs. Stanton. See Foner, *Life and Writings of Frederick Douglass*, pp. 231 – 32, 352, 410, 448 – 54. Ida B. Wells and Mary Church Terrell make reference to their own associations with Susan B. Anthony in their respective autobiographies. See Mary Church Terrell, *Colored Woman in a White World* (Washington, D.C.: Ransdell, Inc., 1940); and Ida B. Wells, *Crusade for Justice*, ed. Alfreda M. Duster (Chicago: University of Chicago Press, 1970).

1. See Kenneth R. Johnson, "Kate Gordon and the Woman Suffrage Movement in the South," *Journal of Southern History* 38 (August 1972): 365 — 92.
2. Ibid., p. 381. The most prominent of the Southern women to join NAWSA was Mrs. Nellie Nugent Somerville of Mississippi, who became its second vice-president in 1915.
3. A detailed discussion of the opportunist character of NAWSA after 1890 will be found in the book by Aileen S. Kraditor, *The Ideas of the Woman Suffrage Movement, 1890 — 1920* (Garden City, N.Y.: Doubleday, Anchor Books, 1971).
4. Rayford W. Logan, *The Negro in the United States: A Brief History* (Princeton, N.J.: D. Van Nostrand Co., 1957), p. 39.
5. August Meier, *Negro Thought in America, 1880 — 1915: Radical Ideologies in the Age of Booker T. Washington* (Ann Arbor: University of Michigan Press, 1963), p. 162.
6. James E. Boyle, "Has The Fifteenth Amendment Been Justified?," *Arena* 31 (May 1904): 488.
7. John C. Wickliffe, "Negro Suffrage A Failure: Shall We Abolish It?," *Forum* 14 (February 1893): 797 — 804; Atticus G. Haygood, "The Black Shadow in the South," ibid. (October 1893): 167 — 75; Charles H. Smith, "Have American Negroes Too Much Liberty," ibid., pp. 175 — 83; J. Montgomery McGovern, "The Race Problem: Disfranchisement As A Remedy," *Arena* 21 (April 1899): 438 — 46; Edgar Gardner Murphy, "Shall the Fourteenth Amendment Be Enforced?," *North American Review* 180 (January 1905): 109 — 33; "Shall the Negro Be Educated?," *Outlook*, May 4, 1901, pp. 13 — 15. This last citation is an editorial in favor of Negro education, but suggests that colored children should be taught more industrial and fewer academic subjects, and that their training should emphasize moral character rather than intellectual pursuits. The *Outlook* editors, moreover, are a far cry from civil-rights advocates of the modern period. They write: "The seven millions of colored persons are going to remain in the South. To deport them is physically impossible. To absorb them by inter-marriage with the Anglo-Saxon race is not thought of as possible by any one whose judgment is determined by facts. . . . They are not dying off, and will not thus disappear from the American continent. They cannot be reduced into a condition of slavery, and no one wishes so to reduce them. What remains? But one alternative: to give them the best education they are capable of receiving, or to leave them to increasing degeneration and decay, a burden and peril alike to themselves and their neighbors . . ." (p. 13).
8. John Bascom, "The Three Amendments," *Annals of the American Academy of Political and Social Science* 27 (May/June 1906): 603.
9. Stephen B. Weeks, "History of Negro Suffrage," *Political Science Quarterly* 9 (December 1894): 680.
10. The Supreme Court decision was quoted in an article by Walter C. Hamm, "Three Phases of Colored Suffrage," *North American Review* 168 (March 1899): 285. A brief discussion of its import will also be

found in Richard Kluger, *Simple Justice: The History of Brown v. Board of Education and Black America's Struggle for Equality* (New York: Alfred A. Knopf, 1976), p. 68.

11. Edgar Gardner Murphy, "Shall the Fourteenth Amendment Be Enforced?," *North American Review* 180 (January 1905): 127.

12. W. E. Burghardt Du Bois, "The Southerner's Problem," *Dial*, May 1, 1905, p. 317.

13. Edward Atkinson, "The Negro A Beast," *North American Review* 181 (July 1905): 202. A detailed examination of the racist literature of this period may be found in George M. Frederickson, *The Black Image in the White Mind: The Debate on Afro-American Character and Destiny, 1817–1914* (New York: Harper and Row, 1971).

14. Black communities were attacked by mobs of white hoodlums in many cities in this period, including Atlanta, Georgia (1906); Springfield, Illinois (1908); East St. Louis (1917); and Chicago (1919). Also, the ghettoization of Harlem and Chicago took place between 1890 and 1920 as the result of a conscious policy executed by city and state officials to enforce "a rigid pattern of discrimination and segregation." See Allan H. Spear, *Black Chicago: The Making of a Negro Ghetto, 1890–1920* (Chicago: University of Chicago Press, 1967), pp. viii–ix, 11–27; and Gilbert Osofsky, *Harlem: The Making of a Ghetto* (New York: Harper and Row, 1965).

15. Ida B. Wells, *A Red Record, Tabulated Statistics and Alleged Causes of Lynchings in The United States, 1892–1893–1894* (1895; reprint ed. New York: New York Times, Arno Press, 1969), p. 9.

16. James Elbert Cutler, *Lynch Law: An Investigation into the History of Lynching in the United States* (New York: Longmans, Green and Co., 1905), p. 161.

17. Walter White, "A Statement of Fact," in *A Documentary History of the Negro People in the United States*, ed. Herbert Aptheker, vol. 2, *From the Emergence of the NAACP to the Beginning of the New Deal, 1910–1932* (Secaucus, N.J.: Citadel Press, 1973), pp. 610–11.

18. Ida B. Wells, *A Red Record*, p. 8.

19. Mary Church Terrell, "Lynching From A Negro's Point of View," *North American Review* 178 (June 1904): 862.

20. Jacquelyn Dowd Hall, *Revolt Against Chivalry: Jessie Daniel Ames and the Women's Campaign Against Lynching* (New York: Columbia University Press, 1979), p. 148.

21. Jane Addams, "Respect for Law," *Independent*, January 3, 1901, pp. 18–20.

22. "Some Negro Views of the Negro Question," *Harper's Weekly*, June 18, 1904, p. 928.

23. "Negro Problem as Discussed By A Colored Woman and Two White Women," *Independent*, March 17, 1904, p. 593.

24. An excellent account of the ASWPL is in the biography of Jessie Daniel Ames by Hall, *Revolt Against Chivalry*.

25. Kraditor, *The Ideas of the Woman Suffrage Movement*, p. 159.

26. W. E. B. Du Bois, *Disfranchisement* (New York: National American Woman Suffrage Association, 1912), p. 10. This pamphlet will be found among the Du Bois Papers located at the University of Massachusetts at Amherst. The speech itself is reprinted in Philip S. Foner,

ed., *W. E. B. Du Bois Speaks: Speeches and Addresses, 1890 – 1919* (New York: Pathfinder Press, 1970), pp. 230 – 38.

27. This was reported in "A Resolution," in *Crisis* 15 (November 1917):21.

28. [W. E. B. Du Bois], "Woman Suffrage," *Crisis* 6 (May 1913): 26 – 29.

29. Du Bois reported on these elections. See "Along the Color Line," *Crisis* 3 (November 1911): 7; "Votes for Women," ibid. 8 (August 1914): 179 – 81; "The Elections," ibid. 9 (December 1915): 79; "Votes for Women," ibid. 15 (November 1917): 1 – 2.

30. Mary Church Terrell Papers, Manuscript Division, Library of Congress, Washington, D.C., Mary Church Terrell, *The Progress of Colored Women* (Washington, D.C.: Smith Brothers Printers, n.d.), p. 7. This is a pamphlet containing the text of Mrs. Terrell's speech.

31. Hallie Quinn Brown, *Homespun Heroines and Other Women of Distinction* (1926; reprint ed., Freeport, N.Y.: Books for Libraries Press, 1971), p. 112.

32. Ida B. Wells, *Crusade for Justice,* ed. Alfreda M. Duster (Chicago: University of Chicago Press, 1970), p. 345.

33. Ida B. Wells, *Southern Horrors. Lynch Law In All Its Phases* (1892; reprint ed., New York: New York Times, Arno Press, 1969), p. 4.

34. Ibid., p. 5.

35. Emma Lou Thornbrough, "The National Afro-American League, 1887 – 1908," *Journal of Southern History* 27 (November 1961): 495.

36. Wells, *Crusade,* p. 64.

37. Wells, Preface to *Southern Horrors,* n.p.

38. Wells, *Crusade,* p. 72.

39. Ibid., p. 78.

40. "Hon. Fred. Douglass's Letter," in Wells, *Southern Horrors,* n.p.

41. Ida B. Wells, ed., *The Reason Why The Colored American is not in the World's Columbian Exposition* (Chicago: Published by the Author, 1893). A copy of this book may be found in the archives of the Library Division of the British Museum in London. (A Xeroxed copy is in my possession.)

42. Cutler, *Lynch Law,* pp. 229 – 30.

43. Alfred S. Johnson, ed., *The Cyclopedic Review of Current History,* vol. 4, *Columbian Annual, 1894* (Buffalo, N.Y.: Garretson, Cox and Co., 1895), p. 647.

44. U.S., Congress, Senate. Senator Lodge presents petitions against lynching from citizens of Boston. Referred to Committee on Education and Labor. *Congressional Record,* 53d Cong., 3d sess., 4 December 1894, 27:15.

45. David M. Tucker, "Miss Ida B. Wells and the Memphis Lynching," *Phylon* 32 (Summer 1971): 121.

46. The initiatives of Black women were significantly advanced with the emergence of the NAACP in 1909 and its campaign against lynching. See Robert L. Zangrando, *The NAACP Crusade Against Lynching, 1909 – 1950* (Philadelphia: Temple University Press, 1980). Unfortunately, Zangrando pays little attention to the role of Black women either in forging the antilynching movement, or in forming the NAACP.

47. Carrie Chapman Catt and Nettie Rogers Shuler, *Woman Suffrage and Politics: The Inner Story of the Suffrage Movement* (New York: Charles

Scribner's Sons, 1923, reprint ed., Seattle: University of Washington Press, 1970), p. 462.

48. U.S., Congress, House. Representative Harrison amending House Joint Resolution 1, proposing an amendment to the Constitution extending the suffrage to women. *Congressional Record*, 65th Congress, 3d sess., 3 June 1919, 57:556.

49. Quoted in Catt and Shuler, *Woman Suffrage and Politics*, p. 464. Du Bois offered an interesting analysis of senatorial opposition to woman suffrage in *Crisis* 8 (June 1914): 77–79.

50. Catt and Shuler, *Woman Suffrage and Politics*, pp. 422–61, tend to underplay the race issue in Tennessee, as does A. Elizabeth Taylor, *The Woman Suffrage Movement in Tennessee* (New York: Bookman Associates, 1957), pp. 75–90. Eleanor Flexner, *Century of Struggle* (Cambridge: Harvard University Press, 1976), in her chapter "Who Opposed Woman Suffrage?" is, I think, closer to the truth on the centrality of the race issue (pp. 304–18).

51. William Pickens, "The Woman Voter Hits the Color Line," *Nation* 6 (October 1920): 273.

52. [W. E. B. Du Bois], "Triumph," *Crisis* 20 (October 1920): 261.

4. "On the Damnation of Women": W. E. B. Du Bois and a Theory for Woman's Emancipation

1. W. E. B. Du Bois, *Darkwater, Voices From Within the Veil* (1920; reprint ed., New York: Schocken Books, 1969), p. 181.

2. Ibid., p. 164.

3. Ibid., pp. 164–65.

4. Ibid., p. 181.

5. Ibid., p. 165.

6. Ibid., p. 163.

7. Ibid., p. 172.

8. Ibid., pp. 172–73, 185.

9. Ibid., p. 181.

10. Ibid., p. 77.

11. Ibid., pp. 79–80.

12. "Suffering Suffragettes," *Crisis* 4 (June 1912): 75–78. See also "Woman's Suffrage Number," ibid. 4 (September 1912), and "Votes for Women: A Symposium By Leading Thinkers of Colored America," ibid. 10 (August 1915). There are some inaccuracies, but a fairly good documentation of Du Bois's coverage of woman's suffrage appears in Jean Fagan Yellin, "Du Bois' *Crisis* and Woman's Suffrage," *Massachusetts Review* 14 (Spring 1973): 365–75.

13. "Hail Columbia!," *Crisis* 6 (April 1913): 289–90.

14. *The Correspondence of W. E. B. Du Bois*, ed. Herbert Aptheker, vol. 1, *Selections, 1877–1934* (Amherst: University of Massachusetts Press, 1973), pp. 209–10.

15. Ibid., pp. 301–2.

16. See W. E. B. Du Bois, ed., *The Negro Church*. Report of a Social Study Made under the direction of Atlanta University; together with the Proceedings of The Eighth Conference for the Study of Negro Prob-

lems, held at Atlanta University, May 26th, 1903 (1903; reprint ed., New York: New York Times, Arno Press, 1968); W. E. B. Du Bois, ed., *The Negro American Family.* Report of a social study made principally by the college classes of 1909 and 1910 of Atlanta University ... together with the Proceedings of the 13th Annual Conference for the Study of Negro Problems, held at Atlanta University, May 26th, 1908 (1908; reprint ed., New York: New York Times, Arno Press, 1968); and W. E. B. Du Bois, ed., *Efforts for Social Betterment among Negro Americans.* Report of a Social Study made by Atlanta University ... together with the Proceedings of the 14th Annual Conference for the Study of Negro Problems, held at Atlanta University, May 24th, 1909 (1909; reprint ed., New York: New York Times, Arno Press, 1968).

17. Gregory V. Rigsby, Foreword to *The Quest of The Silver Fleece,* by W. E. Burghardt Du Bois (1911; reprint ed., New York: New York Times, Arno Press, 1969), p. 2.

18. *Crisis* 2 (July 1911): 100; ibid. 4 (August 1912): 196 – 97; ibid. 5 (September 1912): 237 – 39.

19. Ibid. 7 (July 1914): 117 – 18; ibid. 8 (February 1915): 169 – 70; ibid. 7 (August 1914): 171.

5. Quest for Dignity: Black Women in the Professions 1865 – 1900

1. Anna Julia Cooper, *A Voice From the South By a Black Woman of the South* (1892; reprint ed., New York: Negro Universities Press, 1969), pp. 73 – 74. These are the figures as Cooper reported them in 1892: "Fisk leads the way with twelve; Oberlin next with five; Wilberforce, four; Ann Arbor and Wellesley three each; Livingston two; Atlanta one; and Howard, as yet none."

2. W. E. B. Du Bois and Augustus Dill, eds., *The College-Bred American Negro.* Report of a Social Study made by Atlanta University under the patronage of the Trustees of the John F. Slater Fund; with the Proceedings of the 15th Annual Conference for the Study of the Negro Problems, held at Atlanta University on May 24, 1910 (Atlanta: Atlanta University Press, 1910).

3. Kelly Miller, "The Historic Background of the Negro Physician," *Journal of Negro History* 1 (April 1916): 106.

4. Quoted by Herbert Morais, *The History of the Negro in Medicine* (New York: Publishers Company, Inc., 1967), p. 226. See also Rayford W. Logan, "The Evolution of Private Colleges for Negroes," *Journal of Negro Education* 27 (Summer 1958): 213 – 20; and Horace Mann Bond, "The Origin and Development of the Negro Church-Related College," ibid. 29 (Summer 1960): 217 – 26; and "Meharry Medical College," *Opportunity* 2 (April 1924): 122 – 23.

5. See James L. Curtis, M.D., *Blacks, Medical Schools, and Society* (Ann Arbor: University of Michigan Press, 1971), especially the chapter on "Historical Perspectives"; and M. Alfred Haynes, "Distribution of Black Physicians in the United States, 1967," *Journal of the American Medical Association* 210 (October 1969): 93 – 95.

6. Mary Roth Walsh, Introduction to Dr. Elizabeth Blackwell, *Pioneer Work in Opening the Medical Profession to Women: Autobiographical*

Sketches (1895; reprint ed., New York: Schocken Books, 1977), p. xi. See also Mary Roth Walsh, *"Doctors Wanted: No Women Need Apply": Sexual Barriers in the Medical Profession, 1835–1975* (New Haven: Yale University Press, 1977).

7. [W. E. B. Du Bois, ed.], *Completing the Work of the Emancipator, Being the Sixth Annual Report of the National Association for the Advancement of Colored People* (New York: NAACP, 1916), p. 10.

8. Martin Kaufman, "The Admission of Women to 19th-Century American Medical Societies," *Bulletin of the History of Medicine* 50 (Summer 1976): 257.

9. Quoted by Morais, *The History of the Negro in Medicine*, p. 69.

10. John S. Haller, Jr., "The Physician Versus the Negro: Medical and Anthropological Concepts of Race in the Late Nineteenth Century," *Bulletin of the History of Medicine* 44 (March/April 1970): 160–61.

11. William A. Hammond, "Woman in Politics," *North American Review* 137 (August 1883): 142. See also Carroll Smith-Rosenberg and Charles Rosenberg, "The Female Animal: Medical and Biological Views of Woman and Her Role in Nineteenth-Century America," *Journal of American History* 60 (September 1973): 332–56; and Vern Bullough and Martha Voght, "Women, Menstruation and Nineteenth-Century Medicine," *Bulletin of the History of Medicine* 47 (January/February 1973): 66–82.

12. Jacquelyne Johnson, "Black Women in a Racist Society," in *Racism and Mental Health*, ed. Charles V. Willie et al. (Pittsburgh: University of Pittsburgh Press, 1973), pp. 236–37. See also Alan L. Sorkin, "Education, Occupation, and Income of Nonwhite Women," *Journal of Negro Education* 41 (Fall 1972): 345; and Joseph R. Houchins, "The Negro in Professional Occupations in the United States," *Journal of Negro Education* 22 (Summer 1953): 405–10.

13. Gerda Lerner, ed., *Black Women in White America: A Documentary History* (New York: Pantheon Books, 1972), pp. 85–86.

14. Quoted by Dorothy B. Porter, "Sarah Parker Remond, Abolitionist and Physician," *Journal of Negro History* 20 (July 1935): 293.

15. Frederick C. Waite, *History of the New England Female Medical College, Boston* (1950), p. 88, quoted in Walsh, *"Doctors Wanted,"* pp. 61–62.

16. The first two Native American Indian women to receive medical degrees were also graduated from the Woman's Medical College in Philadelphia. They were Dr. Susan LaFlesche Picotte of the Omaha Tribe, in 1889, and Dr. Lillie R. Minoka-Hill of the Mohawk people, in 1899. See Esther Pohl Lovejoy, *Women Doctors of the World* (New York: Macmillan Co., 1957), p. 121.

17. Monroe A. Majors, *Noted Negro Women: Their Triumphs and Activities* (1893; reprint ed., Freeport, N.Y.: Books for Libraries Press, 1971), title page. See also pp. 117, 148, 181, 241, 242, 269, 311, 324, 336, 354.

18. See, for example, "E. Mae McCarroll, A.B., M.D., M.S.P.H., 1898–, First Lady of the NMA," *Journal of the National Medical Association* 65 (November 1973): 544–45. Dr. McCarroll has been a member of the NMA since 1929. She was awarded a special plaque at the Seventy-eighth Annual Convention of the NMA in August 1973.

19. Letter from Booker T. Washington to Halle Tanner Dillon, April 16,

1891, and letter from Halle Tanner Dillon to Booker T. Washington, August 20, 1891, in *The Booker T. Washington Papers*, ed. Louis R. Harlan, vol. 3, *1889–95* (Urbana: University of Illinois Press, 1974), pp. 136–37, 164–65.

20. Some helpful articles detailing this activity are Elliott M. Rudwick, "A Brief History of Mercy-Douglass Hospital in Philadelphia," *Journal of Negro Education* 20 (Winter 1951): 50–66; W. Montague Cobb, "Not to the Swift: Progress and Prospects of the Negro in Science and the Professions," ibid. 27 (Spring 1958): 120–26; Andrew A. Sorensen, "Black Americans and the Medical Profession, 1930–1970," ibid. 41 (Fall 1972): 337–42; "Negro Physicians of Baltimore," *Opportunity* 1 (May 1923): 21–22; Marion M. Torchia, "The Tuberculosis Movement and the Race Question, 1890–1950," *Bulletin of the History of Medicine* 49 (Summer 1975): 152–68; and Morais, *The History of the Negro in Medicine*, esp. chaps. 5, 6, and 8.

21. Maritcha R. Lyons, "Dr. Susan S. McKinney Steward," in *Homespun Heroines and Other Women of Distinction*, ed. Hallie Quinn Brown (1926; reprint ed., Freeport, N.Y.: Books for Libraries Press, 1971), p. 162. See also Leslie L. Alexander, M.D., "Susan Smith McKinney, M.D., 1847–1918. First Afro-American Woman Physician in New York State," *Journal of the National Medical Association* 67 (March 1975): 173–75.

22. W. E. B. Du Bois, "The Races Congress," *Crisis* 2 (September 1911): 200–209. Excerpts from Dr. Steward's paper appear in ibid. 2 (November 1911): 33–34.

23. Lyons, "Dr. Susan S. McKinney Steward," in Brown, *Homespun Heroines*, p. 163.

24. Mabel Keaton Staupers, "The Negro Nurse in America," *Opportunity* 15 (November 1937): 339. See also "Educational Facilities for Colored Nurses and Their Employment," *Public Health Nursing* 17 (April 1925): 203–4.

25. Staupers, "The Negro Nurse in America," p. 339.

26. Fannie Eshleman and Marian L. Dannenberg, "Tuberculosis Training for Colored Student Nurses," *Public Health Nursing* 15 (June 1923): 301. See also Franklin O. Nichols, "Opportunities and Problems of Public Health Nursing Among Negroes," ibid. 15 (March 1924): 121–23; Robert McMurdy, "Negro Women As Trained Nurses, Experiment of a Chicago Hospital," *Survey* 31 (November 1913): 159–60; and Ruth A. Dodd, "Training Negro Nurses," ibid. 45 (March 1921).

27. See, for example, Sarah B. Meyers, "The Negro Problem As It Appears To A Public Health Nurse," *American Journal of Nursing* 19 (January 1918): 278–81; and Ann Doyle, "Rural Nursing Among Negroes," *Public Health Nursing* 12 (December 1920): 981–85.

28. Anna B. Coles, "The Howard University School of Nursing in Historical Perspective," *Journal of the National Medical Association* 61 (March 1969): 113.

29. Elizabeth Jones, "The Negro Woman in the Nursing Profession," *Messenger* 7 (July 1923): 765.

30. Stephen J. Lewis, "The Negro in the Field of Dentistry," *Opportunity* 2 (July 1924): 207.

31. I am grateful to Mrs. Alfreda M. Duster of Chicago for this information.

Mrs. Duster, the youngest daughter of Ida B. Wells, knew Dr. Officer and her family. Dr. Officer's husband was also a dentist, and did practice his profession. (Conversation with Mrs. Duster in Chicago, July 1980.)

32. "Woman Pharmacist Opens Drug Store," *New York Age*, June 4, 1921, p. 1.
33. Sidney Kaplan, *The Black Presence in the Era of the American Revolution, 1770—1800* (Washington, D.C.: New York Graphic Society, Ltd. in association with the Smithsonian Institution Press, 1973), pp. 210—11.
34. Edward T. James and Janet Wilson James, eds., *Notable American Women, 1607—1950. A Biographical Dictionary* (Cambridge: Harvard University Press, 1973), 3:121.
35. Ibid.
36. S. C. Evans, "Mrs. Mary Ann Shadd Cary," in Brown, *Homespun Heroines*, pp. 95—96.
37. Lerner, *Black Women in White America*, p. 324.
38. Georgiana R. Simpson (1866—1944) also received a Ph.D. in 1921, from the University of Chicago in modern languages. She was fluent in French and German, and spent most of her academic life as a professor at Howard University. Eva Dykes received her Ph.D. that same year from Radcliffe, in philosophy. She taught English literature at Howard University and at Oakwood College. In 1925, Anna Julia Cooper was awarded the Ph.D. in Latin, from the Sorbonne in Paris.
39. Cooper, *A Voice from the South*, pp. 144—45.

6. Domestic Labor: Patterns in Black and White

1. The best factual history of domestic labor in the United States is by David M. Katzman, *Seven Days A Week: Women and Domestic Service in Industrializing America* (New York: Oxford University Press, 1978). An excellent Marxist analysis of domestic workers is offered by Susan M. Strasser, "Mistress and Maid, Employer and Employee: Domestic Service Reform in the United States, 1892—1920," *Marxist Perspectives* 1 (Winter 1978): 52—67. Strasser's work was particularly important in the preparation of this essay.
2. The anthropological and historical literature on this male proprietorship over women is vast. In the Marxist classics the argument was first made by Frederick Engels, *The Origin of the Family, Private Property and the State* (1884; reprint ed., New York: International Publishers, 1973). Especially helpful in this edition is the introduction by Eleanor Burke Leacock.
3. Ella Baker and Marvel Cooke, "The Bronx Slave Market," *Crisis* 42 (November 1935): 330—31; reprinted in *A Documentary History of the Negro People in the United States*, ed. Herbert Aptheker, vol. 3, *From the Beginning of the New Deal to the End of the Second World War, 1933—1945* (Secaucus, N.J.: The Citadel Press, 1974), p. 203.
4. Lita Bane, "What's New in Homemaking?," *Ladies' Home Journal*, March 1930, p. 29; cited by Joann Vanek, "Housewives as Workers," in *Women Working: Theories and Facts in Perspective*, ed. Ann H.

Stromberg and Shirley Harkess (Palo Alto, Calif.: Mayfield Publishing Co., 1978), p. 398.

5. Naomi Ward, "I Am A Domestic," *New Masses* 35 (June 1940): 20−21; reprinted in Aptheker, *A Documentary History*, 3:382−84.

6. I. M. Rubinow and Daniel Durant, "The Depth and Breadth of the Servant Problem," *McClure's Magazine* 34 (March 1910): 582−83. Rubinow offers what was then considered a Marxist view of the "servant problem." He makes no mention of Black women, and there are many typically male supremacist assumptions in the essay.

7. Ruth Schwartz-Cowan, "The 'Industrial Revolution' in the Home: Household Technology and Social Change in the 20th Century," *Technology and Culture* 17 (January 1976): 9.

8. Ibid., pp. 22−23.

9. Many studies have shown that it is not the introduction of household appliances but the employment of women in the work force that determines how much time is spent on housework. See the study of Joann Vanek, "Household Technology and Social Status: Rising Standards and Status and Residence Differences in Housework," *Technology and Culture* 19 (July 1978): 370.

10. See the essay by Batya Weinbaum and Amy Bridges, "The Otherside of the Paycheck: Monopoly Capital and the Structure of Consumption," in *Capitalist Patriarchy and the Case for Socialist Feminism*, ed. Zillah R. Eisenstein (New York: Monthly Review Press, 1979), pp. 190−205.

11. Frederick Engels, Introduction to *Wage Labor and Capital* by Karl Marx (1891; reprint ed., New York: International Publishers, 1933), p. 6.

12. Karl Marx, *Capital*, vol. 1, *A Critical Analysis of Capitalist Production* (1887; reprint ed., New York: International Publishers, 1967), p. 168.

13. Mary Anderson, "The Plight of Negro Domestic Labor," *Journal of Negro Education* 5 (January 1936): 66.

14. Baker and Cooke, "Bronx Slave Market," pp. 198−99.

15. Cited by Katzman, *Seven Days a Week*, p. 12 (my emphasis).

16. Ibid., p. 16.

17. Karl Marx, *Pre-Capitalist Economic Formations* (New York: International Publishers, 1964), p. 95. This work was written by Marx in 1857−1858, prior to the writing of *Capital*, but it was not published until 1939−1941. The essay contains many scattered, probably unintentional, but nonetheless provocative, insights relevant to the oppression of women.

18. Katzman, *Seven Days a Week*, p. 15.

19. Ibid., p. 8.

20. Alice Childress, *Like One of the Family: Conversations From A Domestic's Life* (Brooklyn, N.Y.: Independence Publishers, 1955), pp. 1−3.

21. "More Slavery At the South," by a Negro nurse, *Independent* 72 (January 1912): 196−200; reprinted in *Black Women in White America: A Documentary History*, ed. Gerda Lerner (New York: Pantheon Books, 1972), pp. 227−28; also cited by Katzman, *Seven Days a Week*, pp. 24−26.

22. Mary Bularzik, "Sexual Harassment at the Workplace: Historical Notes," *Radical America* 12 (July-August 1978): 25−44. It should be

noted that the term "sexual harassment," however, is a modern one and was first developed by women lawyers in the 1970s in their efforts to find a suitable language in suits filed on behalf of female clients. See Catharine A. MacKinnon, *Sexual Harassment of Working Women: A Case of Sex Discrimination* (New Haven: Yale University Press, 1979).

23. Karen Lindsey, "Sexual Harassment on the Job," *MS. Magazine*, November 1977, pp. 47–48.

24. An excellent statistical breakdown illustrating this job segregation will be found in *Fact Sheets on Institutional Sexism*, prepared by the Council on Interracial Books for Children, 1841 Broadway, New York City, 10023, January 1979. See also Heidi Hartmann, "Capitalism, Patriarchy and Job Segregation by Sex," *Signs* 1 (Spring 1976), and reprinted in Eisenstein, *Capitalist Patriarchy*, pp. 206–47.

25. Michelle Patterson and Laurie Engelberg, "Women in Male Dominated Professions," in Stromberg and Harkess, *Women Working*, p. 179.

26. See Robert W. Smuts, *Women and Work in America* (1959; reprint ed., New York: Schocken Books, 1971).

27. This was presented as an example by a participant in a panel on "Stereotypes of Black Professional Women," at "The Black Woman: Her Past, Present and Future," a conference coordinated by the Africana Studies and Research Center, Purdue University, West Lafayette, Indiana, April 1, 1979.

28. Elizabeth Ross Haynes, "Negroes in Domestic Service in the U.S.," *Journal of Negro History* 8 (October 1923): 435–36.

29. Ibid., p. 414.

30. See the article by Dora Jones, "Self-Help Program of Household Employees," *Afra-American Woman's Journal*, Summer-Fall 1941, pp. 26–29. *Afra-American Woman's Journal* was published by the National Council of Negro Women from 1940–1948. A complete run is available in the council's archives in Washington, D.C.

31. Edith Sloan, "A Time To Act," *NCHE News*, no. 3, September/October 1972. See also "Housework— In the National Interest, A Bill of Rights for Homemakers," *Ms. Magazine*, October 1979, p. 83.

32. This appears to have been the main tactic of the Industrial Workers of the World as far back as 1917. See the letter from Jane Street, a member of the IWW in Denver, Colorado, to Mrs. Elmer Buse of Tulsa, Oklahoma, reprinted by Daniel T. Hobby, ed., "We Have Got Results: A Document on the Organization of Domestics in the Progressive Era," *Labor History* 17 (Winter 1976): 103–8. See also the article by David M. Katzman, "Domestic Service: Woman's Work," in Stromberg and Harkess, *Women Working*, pp. 389–90; and Meredith Tax, *The Rising of the Women: Feminist Solidarity and Class Conflict, 1880–1917* (New York: Monthly Review Press, 1980), esp. chap. 6, "Rebel Girls and the IWW."

7. The Matriarchal Mirage: The Moynihan Connection in Historical Perspective

1. See Daniel P. Moynihan, *The Negro Family: The Case for National Action* (Washington, D.C.: U.S. Government Printing Office, 1965).

2. Charles E. Silberman, *Crisis in Black and White* (New York: Random House, 1964), p. 94.

3. See Angela Y. Davis and Bettina Aptheker, eds., *If They Come in the Morning: Voices of Resistance* (New York: New American Library, 1971), esp. Angela Davis, "Political Prisoners, Prisons and Black Liberation"; and Bettina Aptheker, "The Social Functions of the Prisons in the United States"; and the cases of Ericka Huggins, the Panther 21, Connie Tucker, Norma Gist, and Marie Hill.

4. For an excellent study on forced sterilization in Latin America, which includes much data on the United States, see Bonnie Mass, *Population Target: The Political Economy of Population Control in Latin America* (Toronto: Women's Press, 1976).

5. See the essay by Angela Davis, "Reflections on the Black Woman's Role in the Community of Slaves," *Black Scholar* 3 (December 1971): 2 – 16.

6. Frederick Douglass, "Lecture on Slavery," Rochester, New York, December 8, 1850; reprinted in Philip S. Foner, ed., *The Life and Writings of Frederick Douglass*, vol. 2, *Pre-Civil War Decade* (New York: International Publishers, 1950), p. 142.

7. Joyce A. Ladner, *Tomorrow's Tomorrow: The Black Woman* (Garden City, N.Y.: Doubleday, Anchor, 1972), p. 46.

8. Herbert G. Gutman, "Persistent Myths about The Afro-American Family," *Journal of Interdisciplinary History* 6 (Autumn 1975): 200. See also Frank F. Furstenberg, Theodore Hershberg, and John Modell, "The Origins of The Female-Headed Black Family: The Impact of the Urban Experience," ibid. 6 (Autumn 1975): 211 – 33; W. E. B. Du Bois, *The Philadelphia Negro* (1898; reprint ed., Millwood, N.Y.: Kraus-Thomson Organization, Limited, 1973); Charles V. Willie, ed., *The Family Life of Black People* (Columbus, Ohio: Charles B. Merrill, 1970).

9. Davis, "Reflections on the Black Woman's Role in the Community of Slaves," p. 7.

10. Claudia Goldin, "Female Labor Force Participation: The Origin of Black and White Differences, 1870 and 1880," *Journal of Economic History* 37 (March 1977): 87.

11. Lorenzo J. Greene and Carter G. Woodson, *The Negro Wage Earner* (Washington, D.C.: Association for the Study of Negro Life and History, 1930), p. 173. See also "Negro Women in South Carolina Industries," *Opportunity* 2 (May 1924): 146 – 47; Helen B. Sayre, "Negro Women in Industry," ibid. 2 (August 1924): 242 – 44; Elizabeth Ross Haynes, "Two Million Negro Women at Work," *Southern Workman* 5 (1922): 64 – 72; "Employment of Colored Women in Chicago," *Crisis* 1 (January 1911): 24 – 25; and Jean Collier Brown, "The Economic Status of Negro Women," *Southern Workman* 60 (1931): 428 – 37.

12. Minnie Miller Brown, "Black Women in Agriculture," *Agricultural History* 50 (January 1976): 211.

13. Elizabeth M. Almquist and Juanita L. Wehrle-Einhorn, "The Doubly

Disadvantaged: Minority Women in The Labor Force," in *Women Working: Theories and Facts in Perspective*, ed. Ann H. Stromberg and Shirley Harkess (Palo Alto, Calif.: Mayfield Publishing Co., 1978), p. 70.

14. Brown, "Black Women in Agriculture," p. 210. See also R. R. Campbell, D. M. Johnson, and G. Strangler, "Return Migration of Black People to the South," *Rural Sociology* 34 (Winter 1974): 504 – 28.

15. These figures come from the United States Department of Commerce, 1978, and were compiled in *Fact Sheets on Institutional Sexism*, by the Council on Interracial Books for Children, New York, January 1979.

16. Robert W. Smuts, *Women and Work in America* (New York: Columbia University Press, 1959), p. 105.

17. Esther Peterson, "Working Women," *Daedalus* 93 (Spring 1964): 685, 688.

18. Ibid., p. 688.

19. Brown, "Black Women in Agriculture," p. 204.

20. Sabina Martinez, "Negro Women in Organization—Labor," *Aframerican* 2 (Summer/Fall 1941): 17; excerpted in *Black Women in White America: A Documentary History*, ed. Gerda Lerner (New York: Pantheon Books, 1972), pp. 263 – 64.

21. See Mindy Thompson, *The National Negro Labor Council: A History*, Occasional Paper, no. 27 (New York: The American Institute for Marxist Studies, 1978), pp. 37 – 42.

22. An excellent history of this strike is provided by Akosua Barthwell, *Trade Unionism in North Carolina: The Strike against Reynolds Tobacco, 1947*, Occasional Paper, no. 21 (New York: The American Institute for Marxist Studies, 1977).

23. Ibid., p. 6.

24. See J. H. O'Dell, "Charleston's Legacy to the Poor People's Campaign," *Freedomways* 9 (Summer 1969): 197 – 211.

25. Ibid., p. 208.

26. Ida Louise Jackson, "The National Non-Partisan Council on Public Affairs," *Opportunity* 20 (November 1942): 327 – 29. See also the Papers of Mrs. Mary C. Gregory and Series 5, Folder No. 133, at the National Archives for Black Women's History, at the National Council of Negro Women, Washington, D.C.

27. See Gladys Byram Shepperd, *Mary Church Terrell: Respectable Person* (Baltimore: Human Relations Press, 1959).

28. See Gloria Richardson, "Focus on Cambridge," *Freedomways* 4 (Winter 1964): 28 – 34; Septima P. Clark, "Literacy and Liberation," ibid., pp. 113 – 24; Mae Mallory, "Memo From A Monroe Jail," ibid. (Spring 1964): 203 – 14; Howard Zinn, *SNCC: The New Abolitionists* (Boston: Beacon Press, 1964); National Archives for Black Women's History, National Council of Negro Women, Washington, D.C. The WIMS material has not yet been processed, but should be available in 1983.

29. Eleanor Holmes Norton, "The Woman Who Changed the South: A Memory of Fannie Lou Hamer," *MS. Magazine*, June 1977, p. 98. See also J. H. O'Dell, "Life in Mississippi: An Interview With Fannie Lou Hamer," *Freedomways* 5 (Spring 1965): 231 – 42; and Laurence Guyot and Mike Thelwell, "The Politics of Necessity and Survival in Mississippi," ibid. 6 (Spring 1966): 120 – 32.

Index

Library of Congress Cataloging in Publication Data
Aptheker, Bettina
Woman's legacy.
Includes index.
1. Afro-American women. 2. United States—Race
relations.   I. Title.
E185.86.A67   305.4'8   81 — 23137
ISBN 0 — 87023 — 364 — 5   AACR2
ISBN 0 — 87023 — 365 — 3 (pbk.)